# AN INTRODUCTION TO THE PRISON EPISTLES

**Introduction**
There are four letters in the New Testament that were written by Paul during a period of imprisonment in Rome and which are commonly called the Prison Epistles. He had been imprisoned before (for two years in Caesarea – Acts 24:27; cf. 2 Cor 6:5) and would be imprisoned again just before his death.  That Paul was imprisoned is evident from his language. In Ephesians he refers to himself as the "prisoner of Jesus Christ" (Eph. 3:1; 4:1); in Colossians he speaks of a "fellow prisoner" called Aristarchus (Col. 4:10); in Philippians he refers to his "bonds" (Phil. 1:7, 13, 14 and 16). In Philemon he refers to himself as "Paul the aged and now also a prisoner of Jesus Christ" (Phm. 9).

**Philemon and Colossians**
Philemon was plainly written at the same time as Colossians since both refer to Onesimus (Col. 4:9) the runaway slave whom Philemon had owned (Col. 4:7-9; Phm 10-12) and whom Paul sends back with Tychicus from Rome to Colossae. Philemon somewhat strangely is not placed alongside Colossians in the canon but with the letters to Timothy and Titus which were written some time later. The order in which the Prison Epistles appear seems to be decided by their length.

**Ephesians and Colossians**
Ephesians bears a strong resemblance to Colossians and vice versa. The practical sections of the epistles are very similar. Ephesians deals with the obligations of wives, husbands, children and slaves (Eph. 5:22-6:9) and so does Colossians (Col. 3:18-4:1).  The instructions given are very similar.  In the closing greetings two passages (Eph. 6:21-22 and Col. 4:7-9) are virtually identical.

Both Ephesians and Colossians devote a great deal of space to the pre-eminent status of the Lord Jesus. Whereas the Gospel writers set out what He did and said and do not devote much space to expounding the theological implications of His life, the Ephesian and Colossian letters along with other New Testament epistles devote themselves to the task of explaining who He is. Philippians, as we shall see, takes up this task but does so in a different way. Ephesians and Colossians have strong similarities in this connection. Both emphasise that He is the "head" of the church.

Philippians as we shall see takes up this task but does so in a different way. Ephesians and Colossians have strong similarities in this connection. Both emphasise that He is the "head" of the church (Eph. 4:15; 5:23; Col. 1:18; 2:19). The purpose is to show that Christ has supreme authority over the Church and is in close communion with the individual believers which form part of it. Both Ephesians and Colossians describe Him as the "fullness". Why Paul did so is a matter of debate.[1]   But the underlying point is clear. He does not require to be supplemented by anyone or anything else. He is the all-sufficient Saviour (Eph 1:22-23; 4:13; Col. 1:19; 2:9).

The letters are also bound together by phraseology not found elsewhere. He speaks of the unsaved as "alienated" (Eph. 2:12; 4:18 and Col. 1:21), he tells believers to "redeem the time" (Eph. 5:16 and Col. 4:5) and describes them as "rooted" (Eph. 3:17 and Col. 2:7). He describes the gospel as "the word of truth, the gospel" (Eph. 1:13 and Col. 1:5) and uses some distinctive wording to describe their links with Christ and one another e.g. "held together," "supply" (Eph. 4:16 and Col. 2:19).

There are some important differences as well. He had been to Ephesus and had planted the church there. He had never been to Colossae (Col. 2:1). He does not refer to individuals by name in Ephesians. Some have supposed therefore that the letter was a circular destined for a number of churches. Colossians by contrast has long list of people to whom he sends greetings in ch4. In Colossians when Paul speaks of the church he refers to the local assembly whereas in Ephesians the Church is the whole body of believers, sometimes for the sake of clarity called the Universal Church. No particular doctrinal problem seems to be on Paul's mind in the Ephesian letter whereas in Colossae there are clear references to the problems caused by Jews who were seeking to promote the use of the ceremonial law and also introduce Greek philosophical ideas.

Paul's situation had moved on from that recorded in Acts 28:30 in this letter. When Luke completed Acts, Paul was in rented accommodation in Rome awaiting trial. In Phil. ch 1:12-13 he is no longer in a hired house but in the Praetorian which was

---

[1]Some consider that Paul was using the language of a philosophical and religious system of belief called Gnosticism which emphasized knowledge of hidden secrets as the means of obtaining full knowledge or enlightenment.

part of the Emperor's palace. This may mean that as his appeal/trial drew on and legal procedure began to occur he was taken into closer custody.

## Philippians

Philippians is organised in a different way from Ephesians and Colossians. Whereas they are divided into two sections one doctrinal and the other practical, Philippians mingles the doctrinal and practical. Unlike the Ephesian and Colossian letters there is a strong autobiographical element in Philippians. In ch 1 he discusses his present predicament in the Praetorian Guard's prison and in ch 3 reflects on his Jewish upbringing. He also spends time discussing his relationship with the church in Philippi and their longstanding loyalty to him. These features are absent in Ephesian and Colossians.

Philippians also has a strong emphasis on the humanity of Christ. Arguably the best-known passage of scripture concerning Christ's humanity is in ch 2 where he speaks of the One who "took upon Him the form of a servant" (v7) and has now been "given a name which is above every name" (v9). Ephesians and Colossians focus on the deity of Christ whereas Philippians concentrates on His humanity and the glorification of the man Christ Jesus to God's right hand.

## The Other Prison Epistle

There are of course two other "prison epistles". Philemon, as we will see, accompanied Colossians and has strong links to Ephesians and Philippians. 2 Timothy was also written from prison (2 Tim. 1:8). It does not appear however that this is the same imprisonment. The Acts of the Apostles ends with Paul in Rome and about to have his appeal heard by Caesar (Acts 28:16). It would seem he is under a form of house arrest (Acts 28:30). It follows from 1 Timothy and Titus that he must have been liberated since he refers to visits to towns which he had not visited during the period covered by the Acts (1 Tim. 1:3; Titus 1:5; 3:12), or which cannot be fitted into the chronology of the Acts of the Apostles e.g. 2 Tim 4:13. In 2 Timothy however he is back in prison and anticipating his execution (2 Tim. 4:6).

## KEY SCRIPTURES

13  Till we all come in the unity of the faith, and of the knowledge of
the Son of God, unto a perfect man, unto the measure of the
stature of the fulness of Christ:

**Eph 4:13**

19  For it pleased *the Father* that in him should all fulness dwell;

**Col 1:19**

9   For in him dwelleth all the fulness of the Godhead bodily.

**Col 2:9**

## ??? KEY QUESTIONS

1. How many letters did Paul write from prison?

2. What information in Philemon suggests that Onesimus was a runaway slave?

3. What are the practical implications of Christ being the head of the church?

4. Why is it commonly thought that Ephesians and Colossians were written at about the same time?

# INTRODUCTION TO THE LETTER TO THE PHILIPPIANS

## When was it written?

This letter was probably written towards the end of Paul's imprisonment in Rome in AD 61. Acts 28 ends with Paul under house arrest (*custodia libera*).  However in Philippians he seems to have moved his accommodation to the quarters of the Praetorian Guard (1:13).  If his appeal had commenced or a verdict was imminent, he may have been kept in close confinement in the Praetorian because (a) it was convenient to the palace where the appeal was heard or (b) prisoners awaiting a verdict were kept in close confinement near the Court to prevent a flight risk.

## What are its distinctive features?

It is Pithy. Philippians is (probably) the most frequently quoted New Testament book. Scarcely a Breaking of Bread goes by without ch 2:5-11 being mentioned. The book abounds with aphorisms, (short, sharp statements of truth) that are used on greetings cards, sympathy cards, bookmarks wherever there are Christians. Here are some examples  -

**Key Points**
- For to me to live *is* Christ, and to die *is* gain - 1:21
- With Christ; which is far better: - 1:23
- Rejoice in the Lord alway: *and* again I say, Rejoice. - 4:4
- The peace of God, which passeth all understanding, shall keep your hearts and minds through Christ Jesus. - 4:7
- I can do all things through Christ which strengtheneth me. - 4:13
- My God shall supply all your need according to his riches in glory by Christ Jesus. - 4:19

Although much quoted, Philippians does not itself quote scripture[2], a rare feature in a New Testament book.  This may be because the Philippians were a Gentile community and not steeped in the Jewish scriptures. It may also be due to the fact that he did not need to invoke the authority of scripture to correct error.

It is Personal. Its two companion epistles, Ephesian and Colossian, are written in a formal style. They open with a statement of doctrinal truth and then they close

---

[2]There is an allusion to Job 13:16 (LXX) in Phil. 1:19.

with practical exhortations. In Philippians the practical and doctrinal are mixed together. We learn more about Paul's background in ch 3 than we do from any other part of the Bible.

<u>It is Political</u>. Philippi was a "colony" (Acts 16:12) of Rome.[3] This meant that it had its own legislature modelled on Roman lines. Its people spoke Latin and dressed as Romans dressed. It used Roman coinage and its citizens had the rights of Romans. This no doubt explains why he used words[4] normally reserved for civil and political rights in connection with the believers' heavenly "citizenship" (1:27; 3:20). Had Paul been writing to a Jewish audience he might have used references to the O.T. or Jewish life to make his points. But in this epistle Paul speaks about the "politics" of the Christian.

<u>It is Practical</u> – Philippians does not introduce any new doctrine. Its most famous passage (2:5-11) dwells on a familiar truth – the humility of the Saviour. It illustrates that truth from familiar facts – His birth and crucifixion. But it expresses these truths in a way designed to help the Christian live. Its main themes such as perseverance in suffering and joy in believing are mainstream Christian truths expounded in other New Testament books.

**What are its Main Themes?**
It is possible to discern a number of themes. Some are mentioned below.

<u>The Salvation in the Gospel</u>
- The fellowship of the gospel – 1:5
- The defence and confirmation of the gospel – 1:7
- The furtherance of the gospel – 1:12
- The defence of the gospel – 1:17
- The life that commends the gospel – 1:27
- The faith of the gospel – 1:27
- The service of the gospel – 2:22
- The basis of the gospel – 3:9
- The labours involved in the gospel – 4:3

---

[3]*Coloniae civium Romanorum* - none of the other colonies mentioned in the NT is described as such e.g. Corinth, Syracuse, Troas, Pisidian Antioch, Lystra and Ptolemais.
[4]*politeuomai* (1:27) - "conversation" (A.V.); *politeuma* (3:20) – "conversation" (A.V.). The word means "citizenship".

In Acts 16 Paul and Silas reached Philippi and preached the gospel. Their labours resulted in the salvation of Lydia and the jailor (Acts 16:14-15, 31-32).  Others were evidently saved and an assembly was planted.[5]  Both of these early converts were hospitable.[6] Generosity seems to have characterised the church (2 Cor. 8:1-5) from that point on.  Paul warns about those who may attack the gospel (3:2; 18) and speaks of the foundational truths of the gospel such as the death and resurrection of Christ (3:10-11) and the righteousness procured through faith (3:9).

The Submissiveness of the Son
Ch 2:5-11 has been called a "hymn". I am not sure whether it is possible to prove that it was sung. But it has a poetic quality. Whether Paul is quoting from another source or had written the section poetically is not stated. It seems to me to be part of the letter and to take its lyrical quality from Paul's appreciation of the sacred nature of its subject.

The "hymn" teaches the deity of Christ.  He was "equal" with God.  Prior to His conception and birth He had chosen to become man, thus teaching His pre-existence. It also teaches His humanity. The phrase "made in the likeness of men" does not refer to the fact that He was a male but to the fact that he was human.[7] The main point is not to make a doctrinal statement about the Lord's divine nature and human nature but to teach that Christ was selfless and humble. He gave up His position of honour to become man. He then submitted to the death of the cross. Roman citizens were exempt from crucifixion. The citizens of Philippi could not have been crucified. But He gave Himself to the cross to set us free.

Because of His willingness to be abased, God the Father has given Him a "name which is above every name". Although at first sight this name appears to be "Jesus" this cannot be so. That name was given by Joseph and Mary at His birth not at His exaltation. The word "name" here may carry the thought of His reputation or it may refer to the use of the word "name" in the Old Testament when applied to God. There the "Name" was shorthand for Jehovah. The Jews so revered the name of Jehovah that they preferred to use the word "Name"

[5]Luke seems to have joined Paul and Barnabas shortly before they arrived in Philippi (Acts 16:10) and remained after Paul and Silas left (Acts 16:40). The use of "we" and "us" in Acts which denotes Luke's presence does not resume until Acts 20:6.
[6]Acts 16:15, 34
[7]Vine New Testament Dictionary - anthropos is used generally, of "a human being, male or female," without reference to sex or nationality, e.g., Matt. 4:4; 12:35; John 2:25.

rather than use word Jehovah. In the New Testament when we find references to Jehovah from the Old Testament this is usually rendered "Lord". Thus the "Name of Jesus" is a reference to the fact that He has a title which is "Lord". The expression "Lord Jesus" acknowledges that He is Jehovah (as to divinity) and "Jesus" (as to His humanity).

The centrality of the Lord Jesus to Christian life is evident in Philippians. The phrase "in the Lord" occurs 9 times, "in the Lord Jesus" once, "in Christ" 7 times and "in Christ Jesus" 5 times. Here are some examples -

- They are in Christ Jesus – 1:1
- They rejoice in Jesus Christ – 1:26 (3:1; 4:4, 10)
- They are encouraged by Christ – 2:1
- They hope in Christ – 2:19, 24
- They may have the mind of Christ – 2:5
- They stand firm in the Lord – 4:2

The Solidarity of the Believers
The Philippian epistle stresses the need for unity. Although a lot of attention is paid to the difficulty between Euodias and Syntyche in 4:2, there is simply insufficient information to justify treating their difference as symptomatic of a broader problem. Paul does not mention any other difficulty in Philippi. The fact that he does not take sides or specify the nature of the problem suggests that it is a personal difficulty. That is not to say that Paul is unconcerned. His repeated use of the word "all" (1:1, 4, 7, 8, 25; 2:17, 26) indicates his concern for the unity of the whole church. But it goes way too far to suggest that the church required "salvation" i.e. deliverance from a divided condition (Phil. 2:12).

The value of unity is conveyed in a variety of Greek words. The most famous of them all is *koinonia*. This is one of the great biblical words. It basically means a sharing together or partnership.

- The fellowship in the gospel – 1:5
- The fellowship[8] in Paul's apostolic ministry – 1:7

---

[8] "Partakers" - *sunkoinoneo* - the prefix *sun* means "with" and joined to the word *koinonia* means to "share with".

- The fellowship of the Spirit – 2:1
- The fellowship of Christ's sufferings – 3:10
- The fellowship of saints' suffering – 4:14
- The fellowship of saints' giving – 4:15

He encourages the Philippians to "walk by the same rule" and "mind the same thing" (3:15).  He refers to Timothy who "served with me in the gospel" (2:22) and Epaphroditus as "my brother, and fellow worker, and fellow soldier" (2:25). The two women who were at odds had formerly "laboured with me" (4:3).  Paul wants to see them "standing firm in one spirit" and striving side by side in the gospel "with one mind" (Phil 1:27).

<u>The Spirit of the Saints</u>
The world longs for happiness.  It finds it in alcohol, sex, drugs and money. The Christian on the other hand finds his joy in the knowledge his sins are forgiven, that his future is secure and that He has God as his comforter and friend. Testimony in Philippi began with Paul and Silas singing hymns at midnight in the "inner prison" after being beaten (Acts 16:23-25). What enabled them to rise above their circumstances? It was their hope in God.  Paul refers to joy and rejoicing repeatedly in Philippians.

- Paul prayed with joy - 1:4
- Paul rejoiced when the gospel was preached whatever the motive - 1:18
- Paul believed that there was a "joy of faith" and a joy in renewing Christian fellowship -1:25–26
- He found joy in the unity of other believers - 2:2
- He found joy in serving other believers - 2:17
- There is mutual joy in sharing the same purpose - 2:18
- There is rejoicing in the deliverance of valued friends - 2:28, 29[9]
- We should "rejoice in the Lord" - 3:1
- We should rejoice in one another - 4:1
- "Rejoice in the Lord alway: *and* again I say, Rejoice" - 4:4
- We can rejoice when other Christians show care for us - 4:10

---

[9]"Gladness" in A.V. is same word as "joy" *charas*.

## The Suffering of the Church

Paul stresses the way that his sufferings serve to advance the gospel (1:12–13). The Philippians must regard suffering, like believing, as a privilege (1:29). They should endure opposition without fear in their fight for the gospel. This suffering mirrors what they have seen and heard about Paul's experience (1:30).

In addition to Paul, Epaphroditus also suffered for the cause of the gospel (2:27). Likewise Christ suffered the excruciating death of the cross to establish the gospel (2:8). Christ's suffering is not only a model of how to suffer; it is an invitation to participate in Christ's sufferings as part of the believer's quest to know him (3:11). Paul can endure suffering (like hunger and poverty; 4:12) through the strength that Christ gives (4:13).

## KEY QUESTIONS

1. Which passage in Philippians stresses the humility of the Lord Jesus and how did He show His humility?

2. How many times does Paul speak about joy in Philippians and what is the source of it?

3. Why is the unity of the local assembly important?

4. What does Philippians have to say about suffering?

# Chapter One

**Key Points**

- Our chief motivation in life should be to honour the Lord Jesus.

- When people we disagree with preach the gospel we should still desire to see their preaching blessed.

- Death is not an enemy for the Christian since to die is to be "with Christ which is far better".

- It is an honour to suffer for the sake of Christ.

**The Fellowship of the Gospel**

Chapter 1 is characterised by the amount of information it contains about Paul and the assembly at Philippi. This emerges as he explains why he is so attached to them. First of all he observes they had been supportive of him from the start (1:5). Paul had brought the gospel to Philippi (Acts 16:12) along with Silas. It would appear that Luke was with them during the time spent there (see the use of "we" and "us" in Acts 16 indicating that the author of Acts was with them). The two conversions mentioned in that chapter both result in offers of hospitality (Acts 16:15, 34). This warm friendship and fellowship seems to have continued after the assembly was planted.

His affection for them very clear (1:3, 7) and made prayer for them a joyful experience (1:4). The letter may well have been written because of their concern about his state in prison and the attitude the Imperial Court had taken to the charge that the gospel he preached was contrary to Roman Law (1:7; Acts 25:8).[10] Unlike other letters there is no indication in Philippians that they were opposed to Paul in any way or had questions about his teaching.

At the end of the letter (4:15) he acknowledges that after he left Philippi they maintained their interest in him by sending money to support his work.   The letter is in part an acknowledgement of another gift sent to him while he was in prison (4:18).

## The Furtherance of the Gospel

The chapter summarises Paul's circumstances in Rome.  He does not say much about his appeal or its prospects of success. He is however concerned about the effect his imprisonment was having on the Christians in Rome. By this time there were assemblies in Rome, the capital of the Roman Empire. But some of the Christians it seems were opposed to Paul and wanted to upset him (1:15, 16).  Generally we should be wary of judging other people's motives. But here it seems Paul knew what their motive was. Paul knew that they were preaching the gospel so as to upset him.  Why they thought Paul would be upset is unspecified. Perhaps they thought that he was only happy if he was preaching? He makes it clear that his main interest is not the motive of the preacher but the proclamation of the gospel (1:18).

The section between vv. 20-26 sets out Paul's *raison d'etre*.  We can learn valuable lessons by examining his motivations. Paul explains that the possibility of death (by execution) does not concern him (1:23) if that is God's will.  He explains that his dominant reason for living is to honour Christ (1:21).  While death involved loss e.g. loss of life for him, loss of his influence for the Philippians (1:24), it also meant gain (1:21). He would gain a reward for his service, he would gain eternal life in its fullest sense, he would gain the presence of the Saviour (1:23).  He explains that he is torn in two.  He in a sense would welcome a guilty verdict

---

[10]Roman Law was tolerant of religion provided it did not undermine Roman interests. It is possible that the issue Paul faced was whether Christianity was an offshoot of Judaism which Roman Law permitted and if it was, whether it undermined the authority of Caesar in any way.

since he would be executed and "depart to be with Christ which is far better" (1:23) but on the other hand the Philippians would be very upset and he would be unable to build up their faith (1:25) by visiting them again.  While he is confident he will return to the Philippians (1:24) which implies that he expects his appeal to be successful, he also acknowledges the possibility of death (1:20). He also regards that as a good outcome.

**The Faith of the Gospel**
At the end of the chapter he gives some explicit teaching.  He instructs the Philippians to live in a way that is consistent with the gospel (1:27) and in particular to be united as they worked to bring the gospel to the world (1:27). In particular he warns them not to be intimidated by their opponents (1:28).  Suffering, as his experience in prison proved, was a privilege since it was endured for the sake of Christ. When he writes that it is "given" to the Christian "to believe" he is not teaching that God gave the faith to believe in the same way that a gift is thrust into the hand of an unsuspecting child.  As He permits suffering to enter the believer's life we may accept it as a gift not a grief. So too He gives us the privilege of believing in Him not merely at conversion but every step of the Christian life thereafter.

 KEY SCRIPTURES

He which hath begun a good work in you will perform *it* until the day of Jesus Christ
_____
                                                                    **Phil 1:6**

For to me to live *is* Christ, and to die *is* gain
_____
                                                                    **Phil 1:21**

I am in a strait betwixt two, having a desire to depart, and to be with Christ; which is far better
_____
                                                                    **Phil 1:23**

**KEY QUOTES**

He is no fool who gives what he cannot keep to gain what he cannot lose.[11]

**Jim Elliott**

True humility is not thinking less of yourself, it is thinking of yourself less.[12]

**CS Lewis**

---

[11]Journal of Jim Elliott 28 October 1949. Killed by Huaorani Indians Ecuador 8 January 1956, Wheaton College, Illinois, collection 277, Box 1, Folder 8.
[12]Mere Christianity.

## KEY QUESTIONS

1. What were Paul's personal circumstances when he wrote Philippians?

2. What is Paul's perspective on death?

3. What form of opposition to Paul did he become aware of while in prison?

4. Paul says it is given to Christians to believe and to suffer. In what way are faith and suffering gifts?

# Chapter Two

**Key Points**

- Pride divides Christians from one another.

- The Lord Jesus' incarnation and death was a display of unparalleled humility.

- Christians who manifest the humility of Christ are a great blessing to an assembly.

- Unity on a personal as well as doctrinal level is crucial to an assembly's wellbeing.

**The Ingredients of Unity (vv1-2)**

The chapter opens with a plea from Paul. His desire is that the assembly should remain united (v 2). Unity covers a variety of matters. An assembly may be united in its beliefs but at variance over personal issues. True unity exists where there is both unity in doctrine and in personal relations. The only overt sign of disunity in the letter is his reference to the rift between Euodias and Syntyche (4:2). Paul does not state what had caused their difference nor does he indicate that the problem went any wider than these two women. But no doubt experience told the apostle that a minor rift can widen and lead to a split in the assembly. Verse 1 lists the characteristics that will preserve unity. These include love for our fellow believers and the supply of help from God through the Spirit. The word "mind" appears frequently in verses 1-8. It means "attitude" or "spirit" as opposed to IQ. The key is to have the proper attitude to one another. If we love our fellow believers and if the Spirit is working among us we can live in unity.

## The Inspiration for Unity (vv3-11)

He then writes about the Lord Jesus and seeks to show that He was characterised by humility (v5). The Lord Jesus was never in assembly fellowship, but He knew that self-sacrifice was necessary in order to bring blessing to others. Thus He was willing to give up the privileges of deity and become a man. As God He could not have known tiredness or hunger, but as a baby and a man He did. Whereas in heaven He was revered as the Son of God, on earth He took on the "form of a servant" i.e. humanity, and endured all its restrictions so that the blessing of others might be procured. The ultimate example of His selflessness was the crucifixion. Although it is strictly unnecessary to his argument, Paul goes on to show that His selfless attitude resulted in recognition and prominence. As a result of His submission to death He was resurrected and exalted and acclaimed as Lord. The restrictions He undertook were temporary and were replaced by exaltation. He had been the Son of God eternally, but as Jesus, the Son of Man He was acclaimed as "Lord" i.e. of the same status as Jehovah.

## The Importance of Unity (vv12-18)

Paul knew that the believers in Philippi had a high regard for him (v18) and as he rejoiced in their faith so they rejoiced in him. He had never had any reason to rebuke them for disobedience (v12). Because they cared for him he knew they would listen to him. While He had not come from heaven nor been crucified, he had given his life sacrificially for the Christians (v17). Some think that the predicament was so severe that the whole church needed "salvation" (v12), but this goes farther than the text of the letter permits. There are problems, but the assembly is not so far gone as to require corporate salvation. Paul's teaching was designed to avert rather than cure a break down of testimony. He teaches them that they should "work out their salvation with fear and trembling". Here he is teaching that they should "work out" the implications of their faith (v17). The proper spirit for Christian living is "fear and trembling" (v12) and an acknowledgement that we are dependent on God (v13). We must aspire to want what He wants and do what He wants. His admonition that they should not quarrel or criticise (v14) gets to the heart of the issue in Philippi. Perhaps Paul knew that if things were not resolved their testimony would be ruined (v15). Unity is therefore an important indicator that an assembly is in a good spiritual state.

**The Interests of Unity (vv19-24)**
Paul knew that the assembly needed support. In these days the churches were widely scattered. There was no network of assemblies and visiting speakers from other assemblies were probably unknown. Paul therefore sought to direct some of those he worked with to the assembly so that they would help it out. Timothy was someone he knew would help them. Although Paul's position in Rome was difficult he knew that it was in the interests of the Philippians that someone should help them. Hence although he would have benefitted if Timothy had remained with him, he proposed to send him to them. This is an example of the selflessness Paul has been writing about.

**The Illustration of Unity (vv25-30)**
In this section Paul informs the Philippians about Epaphroditus who, it seems, had carried a letter (and gift – 4:18) from the Philippians to Paul in Rome ("your messenger" – v 25) but had taken unwell when there. It must have been a serious illness (v27) but he had recovered. He was not it seems an eminent brother since Paul encourages them to give him the respect he deserved (v29). But he was an example from their own company of the attitude that would preserve the assembly from division. He had not put his interests first (v30) and had suffered as a result (v27). He was more anxious about others than himself (v26). These characteristics would if practised by everyone have a unifying influence.

## KEY SCRIPTURES

*Let* nothing *be done* through strife or vainglory; but in lowliness of mind let each esteem other better than themselves

**Phil 2:3**

Let this mind be in you, which was also in Christ Jesus: [6] Who, being in the form of God, thought it not robbery to be equal with God: [7] But made himself of no reputation, and took upon him the form of a servant, and was made in the likeness of men: [8] And being found in [u]fashion as a man, he humbled himself, and became obedient unto death, even the death of the cross.

**Phil 2:5-8**

## KEY SCRIPTURES

[14] Do all things without murmurings and disputings:

**Phil 2:14**

## KEY QUOTES

Unity of mind is not easily cultivated when human beings of disparate backgrounds and temperaments find themselves sharing one another's company, but the resources that make such unity possible are available to the people of Christ in their fellowship with him. [13]

**F. F. Bruce**

A servant of Christ, enjoying much the companionship of Christ, and intensely devoted to Him, was once asked if he could describe his Master in a word. His reply was "Others". Such is the wonderful and beautiful description of Him given us in [Phil. ch. 2] by His greatest servant.[14]

**Willie Trew**

---

[13]Philippians. Understanding the Bible Commentary (Baker Books) p.61.
[14]Notes on Galatians & Philippians (Precious Seed Pub.) p.55.

## KEY QUESTIONS

1. In what way was Epaphroditus an example to the Philippians?

2. In teaching them about the humility of the Lord Jesus what practical outcome was Paul hoping to achieve?

3. In what way was Paul's behaviour a practical example of humility?

4. In what way was the crucifixion an example of humility?

# Chapter Three

**Key Points**

- True righteousness springs from God not personal achievement.

- The Christian may know God and enjoy His power in his life.

- The death and resurrection of Christ display many of the features we should display in our lives.

- The Christian's true home is in heaven.

## Paul's Past (verses 1-9)

It appears from Paul's language (v1 "finally") that he intended to end the epistle at this point. But the issue he wants to end with (the dangers of Jewish teachers) so provokes him that he writes at length about the doctrinal issue at stake.

He had once believed that keeping the Law was the means of salvation. He had persecuted the early Christians because they rejected the Law as the means of justification. His conversion on the Damascus Road led to a complete change of mind. As a result his former colleagues became his sworn enemies. Scripture records several attempts by the Jewish leaders to kill him. His description of them is sharp and critical ("dogs", "evil workers"). While we might struggle to understand why a Christian should speak so about others, it must be remembered that for Paul they represented the "enemies of the cross" (v18). He knew they would kill him if they could and that their goal was to destroy the churches he had established.

So as to explain why these teachers were wrong and should be opposed, Paul sets out the national and religious qualities he had once trusted in (vv. 4-6). He then contrasts these with the righteousness that God gives the believer through faith (v9). He does not deny that man needs to be righteous to enter heaven. He rejects the idea, however, that righteousness is to be found in our deeds. Salvation depends on God attributing His righteousness to us so that our entry into heaven depends on Him and not us.

Paul uses a spiritual balance sheet to describe this state of affairs (v7). All his personal attainments are put in the debit column ("loss") and all the benefits he has through Christ are put in the credit column ("gain" v8). He concludes that the benefits of knowing Christ far exceed the benefits of practising the Law and trying to be externally righteous.

**Paul's Present (verses 10-16)**
In this section, Paul explains the impact of the death and resurrection of Christ. He shows that believers do not need to wait until their physical resurrection to experience God's resurrection power. Although the sufferings, death and resurrection of Christ are in the past and were unique to Christ, Paul yearns to know in his own life some of what Christ went through. Thus while he cannot go through Christ's sufferings, he can suffer for Christ. He cannot die Christ's death, but he can reproduce features of that death e.g. its selflessness, in his own life. He will never be resurrected like Christ but he can experience the power of God in other ways. Finally, he anticipates the day when believers will be raised from the grave and longs that in the here and now he may experience that transforming power.

**"Knowing Him"** – how can a Christian know the Lord Jesus when he has never met Him? While the Lord was on earth His disciples knew Him personally. They watched Him and listened to Him and developed a personal relationship with Him. Paul makes it clear that it is still possible for the believer to know Christ. The knowledge is built up from a number of sources. We can know Him through reading and hearing about Him. But we can also get to know Him through prayer and communion. Because He is a divine person He is not constrained by His physical absence from earth. He can still communicate with us and we can be conscious of His presence and will. So the physical absence of Christ does not prevent us developing a personal knowledge of Him.

**"The power of His resurrection"** – what kind of power is this? It is plainly not physical power. Human power can restart the heart and bring back people from the dead.  But God's power is far beyond that. This power refers to God's supernatural power to accomplish things that are beyond human ability. In particular it refers to God's power to overcome obstacles (such as death) that are insuperable to humans.

**"Fellowship of His sufferings"** – we plainly did not suffer on the cross with Christ. Nor could we contribute anything to the suffering of Christ for sin.  But when we suffer as Christians we suffer for many of the reasons He suffered.  He suffered because of His commitment to God and His love for the truth.  So too should we.  Because He identifies so closely with His people, He suffers with us.  In this sense we have fellowship in His sufferings.

**"Conformity to His death"** – this does not mean that we wish to be crucified or lashed.  Conformity means conformity of purpose and attitude. In our life the features of Christ's death should be apparent. We should "die" to our personal ambitions and desires. We should be conformed to what His death stands for – obedience to God and devotion to the interests of others.

**"Attaining to the resurrection"** – this does not teach that the resurrection of the saint from the dead depends on how good a Christian he has been. All Christians will be raised irrespective of how good or bad they have been.  His point is that we should seek to live out in the present the qualities that we will achieve when we are resurrected.

**"Apprehend that for which I am apprehended of Christ"** – Paul had gone to Damascus to apprehend believers. Instead God apprehended him.  Here he expresses his desire to seize or grasp all that God had in mind for him when he was "arrested" on the Damascus Road.

## Paul's Future (vv. 17-21)
After spelling out the differences between Christianity and the Law, Paul asks the Philippians to trust him. If they followed these teachers they would be rejecting him.  So he asks them to choose. He also points out that to follow them is to turn their back on the cross and the death of Christ. To choose these teachers was to

choose men who were bound for judgement. Although they were not immoral, the type of fleshly desires they pursued were just as bad. They loved earthly achievement and external ritual. This revealed that their desires were fleshly and not spiritual.

Paul then points on the future for the believer. He has been discussing the power of the resurrection and its implications for the believer. Now he anticipates the day when resurrection (or rapture) would actually occur and each believer is given a body like Christ's. Judaism was incapable of offering such a hope.

 KEY SCRIPTURES

I count all things *but* loss for the excellency of the knowledge of Christ Jesus my Lord:

**Phil 3:8**

I press toward the mark for the prize of the high calling of God in Christ Jesus.

**Phil 3:14**

...our [citizenship] is in heaven; from whence also we look for the Saviour, the Lord Jesus Christ:

**Phil 3:20**

## KEY QUOTES

Paul had looked into the mirror of Calvary, and had seen himself reflected in a way which filled his soul with loathing and disgust. Turning away from that sight, he had turned his eyes upon a sight of surpassing beauty and extreme loveliness. His whole vision was henceforth filled with Christ in glory; his heart was His, exclusively and forever. In the presence of such glory, beauty and worth, the world had no attraction and had nothing to give.[15]

**Willie Trew**

The spiritual saint never believes circumstances to be haphazard, or thinks of his life as secular and sacred; he sees everything he is dumped down in as the means of securing the knowledge of Jesus Christ. .... Self-realization leads to the enthronement of work; whereas the saint enthrones Jesus Christ in his work..... The aim of the spiritual saint is "that I may know Him." Do I know Him where I am today? If not, I am failing Him. I am here not to realize myself, but to know Jesus. In Christian work the initiative is too often the realization that something has to be done and I must do it. That is never the attitude of the spiritual saint, his aim is to secure the realization of Jesus Christ in every set of circumstances he is in.[16]

**Oswald Chambers**

---

[15]Precious Seed 1963 vol. 14 Issue 4.
[16]My Utmost for his Highest.

## KEY QUESTIONS

1. What facts does Paul give us about his upbringing in ch 3?

2. How can a Christian "know" the Lord Jesus?

3. What significance does the resurrection of the Lord Jesus have for the Christian?

4. In what way do we share in the sufferings of the Lord Jesus?

# Chapter Four

## Key Points

- Good Christians can fall out with one another.

- Christians who are in the good of God's blessings ought to have a settled joy and contentment in their lives.

- We ought to focus on the spiritual blessings of Christian life and avoid being absorbed with the sins and failures of others.

- As a result of Paul's testimony there were people saved in the household of Caesar.

## Peace in the Assembly
### Verses 1-4

The opening verses of this chapter reveal that two sisters in the assembly were at odds with one another. Since Paul had not been in Philippi for some time, his knowledge of their dispute must have reached his ears from someone else, possibly Epaphroditus. That Paul refers to their dispute in an open letter indicates that it was a serious fall out and was known to the church. It is unlikely that Paul would have revealed a minor dispute in a public letter. It is reasonable to assume that Paul foresaw that this part of the letter would cause embarrassment to these sisters. Evidently, however, their discomfort was not a sufficient reason to remain silent. Sometimes the fear of causing offence can prevent good men from taking action that is necessary to protect the wider interests of the assembly.

If Paul knew what they had fallen out about, he does not say so. It may be that no one really knew. Oftentimes disputes are an accumulation of grudges and misunderstandings. Whatever the position, Paul does not take sides. He simply implores them both to be "of the same mind in the Lord". This implies that submitting to the Lord Jesus was essential if the dispute was to be resolved. Ch 2 emphasises that humility and a willingness to place other people's interests first is a vital ingredient of unity. Ch 3 emphasises that God is able to give the power to overcome great difficulty. No one should underestimate how hard it is for people to "climb down".

Some have thought that the general emphasis on unity in the letter and this specific dispute implies that the spiritual state of the church at Philippi was so bad that the assembly needed "salvation". This is too gloomy a view of matters. Paul does not say that the church was divided. This letter is in very sharp contrast to the letter to the church at Corinth where division was evident. Paul's teaching about unity was probably designed to prevent rather than resolve assembly division.

This section is addressed to the Philippians as a whole and the two women personally. The reference to the "true yokefellow" is probably to the bearer of the letter, Epaphroditus, who Paul hopes will be able to assist in resolving the schism. "These women" is a reference to Euodias and Syntche. Paul's warm commendation of the women demonstrates that good people can fall out. Discord is not confined to worldly or carnal Christians.

## Peace in the Life
## Verses 5-9

The apostle moves to his conclusion with a series of short admonitions. They all relate to one of the letter's themes namely the "mind" or attitude we have towards life. The apostle reminds them that they ought to be joyful. In the world rejoicing usually accompanies material blessing. The Christian's joy derives from spiritual blessing. The world's rejoicing tends to be short-lived. The Christian ought to be joyful at all times. He ought to be buoyed in his spirit by his spiritual blessings. This does not mean that we find suffering a pleasant thing. We are not expected to laugh at funerals. But we can have a resilient "optimism" whatever life may bring. Philippi had witnessed a singular example of this spirit some years before. When Paul and Silas had been beaten and imprisoned, they were overheard singing God's praises in the prison at Philippi at midnight (Acts 16:25). For the Christian there is always a reason to be thankful. In this letter Paul mentions "joy" and "rejoicing" frequently. Among the things that gave him joy was the knowledge that the gospel was being preached even by rivals (1:18) and that the assembly cared for him (4:10).

We should be known for our "moderation". This word has a few shades of meaning including gentleness, kindness and tolerance. We should be known for our tranquillity of spirit. Through prayer we can unburden ourselves to God and that in turn gives us peace. We ought to be occupied with things which produce Christlikeness. It is sometimes said "we are what we eat". But Philippians says "we are what we think". Sometimes we can become preoccupied with the difficulties of life and fail to rest in God's goodness and care for us. Paul suggests that if we depend on God in prayer the restlessness can be exchanged for God's inner peace. He reminds the Philippians that if we spend our time thinking about things that are upsetting or harmful, our spiritual equilibrium will be disturbed. What we think about is to a great degree a matter of choice. He commends the value of being absorbed with that which is for our spiritual blessing.

## Peace in the Prison
**Verses 10-19**
The Philippians had a commendable concern for Paul. They realized that he needed their practical support so they sent one of their number to visit him in the prison in Rome with a gift. How much was given is not specified. Paul obviously appreciated their gift but is keen to stress that he was not dependent on the gift. He had been through thick and thin during his service for God and had come to appreciate that he could trust in God to meet his needs. He compares their gift to one of the sweet savour sacrifices offered under the Law. Although God did not need the offering it nevertheless was sweet to Him. Likewise their gift was a sacrifice that both God and Paul could appreciate.

## Peace in the Soul
**Verses 21-23**
The epistle ends with Paul's customary ascription of praise to God, sometimes called the doxology. His farewell indicates two things. First, that although he is in prison he has Christian company and, second, that there were Christians

in "Caesar's household". This implies that there were Christians in the staff or military guard attached to the Imperial palace. Presumably Paul had spoken to them while in imprisonment and they had been saved.  It is wonderful to think that the gospel had triumphed even through Paul's imprisonment.

 ## KEY SCRIPTURES

Rejoice in the Lord alway: *and* again I say, Rejoice.

**Phil 4:4**

Be careful for nothing; but in every thing by prayer and supplication with thanksgiving let your requests be made known unto God. [7] And the peace of God, which passeth all understanding, shall keep your hearts and minds through Christ Jesus.

**Phil 4:6-7**

But my God shall supply all your need according to his riches in glory by Christ Jesus.

**Phil 4:19**

## KEY QUOTES

The final chapter of the epistle to the Philippians is one of the great discourses on the doctrine of peace, such as Psalm 23 in the Old Testament and John 14 in the New Testament. .... Paul expresses in this chapter his primary concern that the Philippians will experience wonderful peace in their relationship to the Lord and to each other in triumphing over anxiety. In a modern context when many Christians experience anxiety, this chapter becomes an important revelation from God for mental and emotional health in a tension-filled world.[17]

**John F Walvoord**

A modern beatitude states: "Blessed is the person who is too busy in the day to worry and too tired at night to do it." Some psychologists claim that only 8 percent of a person's worries are legitimate. They assert that 40 percent of such anxieties will never happen, that 30 percent are undue self-criticism, that 12 percent are about old decisions, and that 10 percent pertain to health and aging.[18]

**Robert Gromaki**

---

[17]*Philippians: Triumph in Christ* (Moody Press) pp.100-101.
[18]*Stand United in Joy: An Exposition of Philippians* (Kress Christian Publications) p.171.

## ?? KEY QUESTIONS

1. Why is it that good people fall out?

2. Why should assemblies of Christians be keen to support those that preach the gospel and teach the saints?

3. What sort of attitude does this letter recommend to Christians?

4. How did the gospel reach people who were members of Caesar's household?

# INTRODUCTION TO THE LETTER TO THE EPHESIANS

The letter is written to the church in Ephesus, one of the great cities of the ancient world. Ephesus is situated in modern day Turkey. It is now in ruins. But when this letter was written it was home to about 300 000 people and was the chief city in Asia. It housed the Temple of Artemis (Diana), one of the Seven Wonders of the Ancient World. The worship of Diana is a prominent feature of Luke's account (Acts 19:24) of the gospel reaching Ephesus in Acts. Ephesus appears in the Acts of the Apostles, the prison epistles, the letters to Timothy and in the Book of Revelation. As a result we have more information about the church than any other New Testament church. The period spanned covers about 40 years, from Paul's arrival to preach the gospel to John's "letter within a letter" in the book of Revelation.

Ephesians was probably written at the same time as the Colossian letter. See the Introduction for the similarities between the two letters. Hereunder is a summary of the epistle.

**The Church's Privileges -** In the original letter verses 1:3-14 is one long sentence. It sets out the blessings of Christians "in Christ". In order to explain the blessings of the Christian the apostle utilises terminology used to describe Israel's blessings in the O.T. but reworked so as to reveal the superior blessings in Christ.

**Key Points**
- Israel's blessings were tangible and visible and were situated in Canaan (Gen. 15:7; Gen. 26:3; 28:13), the "land flowing with milk and honey" (Ex. 3:8). The Christians' blessings are "in heavenly places" in Christ (1:3).
- God chose Israel for blessing from among the peoples of the earth (Deut. 7:6). The Church was chosen for spiritual blessing in Christ (1:4).
- Israel was adopted as Jehovah's son out of the nations (Ex. 4:22; Rom. 9:4). But the Christian was adopted as a son from eternity (1:5).
- Israel was redeemed from Egypt by the blood of the Passover lamb (Ex. 6:6) whereas Christians were redeemed from their sin by Christ (1:7).
- Israel had an earthly inheritance (Gen. 15:7) whereas the Church has a heavenly inheritance (1:14).

Whereas other letters pursue arguments and answer questions, Ephesians is dominated by prayer and thanksgiving. This section opens with the words

"Blessed be the God and Father of our Lord Jesus Christ, who...". In the sentence that follows the teaching of the apostle is found in the praise he offers.   Likewise the second section 1:15-23 is a prayer and the apostle's teaching is in the prayer he offers.   The last great praise section is 3:14-21 where again there is much to learn from the apostle's thanksgiving.

**The Church's Power -** Verses 1:15-23 are also one long sentence.  The apostle's prayer here is that the Ephesians might appreciate the greatness of the power at their disposal.   The "hope of His calling" refers to the idea that in calling the Christian (to salvation) the believer has a "hope" namely resurrection and exaltation to heaven.  If God could raise Jesus from the dead, what could He do for us? The Lord Jesus is also linked to the Church in a relationship of affection as well as authority.  The Lord Jesus is superior to the angels; but they are not part of the church. Salvation is described a variety of ways.

- The result of God's choice in eternity past – 1:4
- The result of being adopted by God as His child – 1:5
- The status of being accepted by God because of our links with the Beloved – 1:6
- Receiving redemption through the blood of Christ – 1:7
- Receiving forgiveness of sin – 1:7
- Being heir to a heavenly inheritance – 1:11
- Based on trust - 1:13
- Based on belief – 1:13
- Manifested by spiritual life – 2:1
- Identified with Christ in His resurrection and ascension – 1:20; 2:6
- Bestowed by grace through faith – 2:8
- Receiving the promise of Christ by the gospel – 3:6

This section also contains the first reference to a distinctive feature of Ephesians, angels and spirits.  The "principalities and powers" mentioned in v21 refer to great angelic beings, see also 3:10; 6:12. The letter emphasises the malign power of the most notorious fallen angel, the devil (2:2, 6:11) and the "heavenlies" (1:3, 2:6, 16, 3:10, 6:12) a word unique to Ephesians[19] and which describes a realm apart from earth where both God and angels, fallen and unfallen, reside. This emphasis may

---

[19]Though its cognates appear regularly in scripture.

be because Ephesus was the seat of the worship of Artemis or Diana and Paul associated the devil and evil spirits with idolatry. It may also be because there was a form of religion called Gnosticism abroad which emphasised the role of angels.

**The Church's Pardon –** this section (2:1-10) is marked by the sharp contrast it draws between the state of the unsaved man and the saved man. Paul gives a "before and after" for the Christian.  Before salvation, the Ephesians' everyday life was characterised by sin (2:2), but after salvation they were characterised by good works (2:10).  Before they lived as the world lived (2:2), but after they lived for heaven (2:6). Before they were controlled by Satan (2:2), but after they were controlled by God (2:6). Before they were "dead" (2:1), but after they were "alive" (2:5).

The section is also marked by its stress on man's dependence on God for salvation.  His works do not merit salvation (2:8). The state of the religious man (like Paul) with his religious works is no better than that of the pagan man (like the Ephesians).  Just as God raised Christ, so He gives life to the Christian. The initiative of God is propelled by His love for us and His consequent grace and mercy. Because of His grace and mercy He forgives sin.  He forgive those who respond to the gospel in faith (2:8).

**The Church's Partnership**
2:11-22 are largely occupied with the union of Jew and Gentile. Since the audience in Ephesus was Gentile, it was vital that they did not think they had become members of a Jewish sect. He shows that salvation was for them as much as it was for the Jew.  While in the past the Law had made distinctions between Jew and Gentile, Christ had set aside the Law.  He points out that there is no restriction on the scope of the death of Christ (2:13).  The Lord Himself preached to Gentiles and from an early stage the gospel had spread to the Gentile and Jew alike (2:17). There is a strong hint that while the covenants had been with Israel and Judah, the blood of the New Covenant (2:13) had a universal scope. Gentiles and Jews belonged to one kingdom (2:19), one household (2:19), and one temple (2:21). Jew and Gentile were in partnership together.

Ephesians places a great deal of emphasis on the Church, as the totality of all believers and distinct from Israel.  It is described as -

- The body of Christ – 1:23; 4:12
- A man – 2:15
- A temple - 2:21
- A bride/wife – 5:25

## The Church's Prayer

Ch 3. Although he does not supply any details as to when and how God spoke to him, the apostle explains that God had revealed to him that He was now working among both Jew and Gentile (3:3). He had then specially commissioned him to preach to the Gentiles (3:9). He saw this work as having a heavenly dimension (3:11). The Ephesian epistle has wide horizons. Christ again is at the heart of God's purposes. There are many dispensations in Scripture. The final one is the "dispensation of the fullness of the times". The Millennium is the final phase of testimony before the Eternal State when all things are finally subdued to God and Christ. The apostle closes this section with a prayer. His prayers are mingled with praise. He now prays for more practical matters. He desires that they might enjoy the strength which comes from the Spirit. He desires that they might demonstrate in their life the characteristics of the Lord Jesus. Above all he desires that they might have a grasp of the love of Christ.

## The Church's Principles

Ch 4 bridges the doctrinal and the practical. Unity is a practical truth, but if it is to be realised it needs to be based on common principles. Jews would have understood religious unity. They believed in one God. But the Gentiles had been reared in a world of many Gods and religions. The apostle sets out a doctrinal foundation for unity. Although there is a trinity – there is only one Father, one Son and one Spirit. There is one basis of salvation – not many ways to heaven. There is one baptism – although John had baptised, the Church only recognised baptism in the name of Jesus Christ. There is only one expression of testimony, the Church, and there is one doctrinal body, the faith. But unity is maintained by a diversity of gifts given by God.

## The Church's Practice

From 4:17 to the end the apostle develops a series of practical points. The "old man" is what we were before we were saved (Rom. 6:6; Col. 3:9). Although our connection to Adam was ended on conversion, we are still capable of behaving like the "old man". We should live as "new men". We are now linked with Christ and ought to live in line with His character. The Christian's speech should be pure. He should not lie (4:25) or tell doubtful jokes (4:29). He should never speak angrily or haughtily (4:31). He should not be marked by "empty talk" (5:4). Psalms and hymns should be on his lips (5:19). As to his conduct, he should be kind (4:32) and honest (4:28). Immorality (5:3) and drunkenness (5:18) should be alien to him.

## The Church's Pattern

This section 5:22-6:9 closely resembles the corresponding section in Colossians. It has been called a "household code" and sets out the behaviour of Christians in the home. He discusses wives, husbands, children, slaves (who were part of home life) and masters. He links the conduct of spouses with the values of the Church. Wives are to be submissive as the church is submissive to Christ. Husbands are to love their wives as Christ loves the church. This section is intensely practical and easy to understand. It presents none of the challenges to understanding seen in the earlier part of the epistle.

## The Church's Power

Before the closing greetings (6:21-24) Paul uses an extended metaphor. He describes a Roman soldier or gladiator and draws parallels between his weapons and armour and the armaments God has placed at the disposal of the Christian to protect him in an evil world.

 KEY SCRIPTURES

He hath chosen us in him before the foundation of the world, that we should be holy and without blame before him in love:

**Eph 1:4**

In whom we have redemption through his blood, the forgiveness of sins, according to the riches of his grace.

**Eph 1:7**

**KEY SCRIPTURES**

He raised him from the dead, and set *him* at his own right hand in the heavenly *places*, [21] Far above all principality, and power, and might, and dominion, and every name that is named, not only in this world, but also in that which is to come:

**Eph 1:20-21**

By grace are ye saved through faith; and that not of yourselves: *it is* the gift of God:

**Eph 2:8**

*There is* one body, and one Spirit, even as ye are called in one hope of your calling; [5] One Lord, one faith, one baptism, [6] One God and Father of all, who *is* above all, and through all, and in you all.

**Eph 4:4-6**

Walk in love, as Christ also hath loved us, and hath given himself for us an offering and a sacrifice to God for a sweetsmelling savour.

**Eph 5:2**

No NT writing more joyfully celebrates God's grace in the gospel than does Ephesians, nor does any contain so rich and concentrated a vein of theological gold. This short letter's profound and extensive influence on the church's thought, liturgy, and piety ranks with that of the much longer Psalms, John, and Romans. It was Calvin's favourite letter, and Coleridge was later to pronounce it "the divinest composition of man." [20]

**Max Turner**

Unlike many of Paul's other letters, Ephesians was not written to address any particular problem or controversy. Paul wrote the letter to instruct the Christians of Asia Minor concerning the privileges and responsibilities of those who were part of the church, the Body of Christ... The basic theme of Ephesians is the church, the Body of Christ. Christ is the Head, and the Body is made up of believing Jews and Gentiles. The church is a new community purchased by Christ to carry out the purposes of God in this world. [21]

**Paul Benware**

---

[20] Ephesians *Theological Interpretation of the New Testament: A Book-by-Book Survey* (SPCK) p.124.
[21] *Survey of the New Testament* (Moody Press) pp.224-225.

## KEY QUESTIONS

1. In what way do the Church's blessings exceed the blessings given to Israel?

2. When Paul speaks of the "hope" of the Christian what is he referring to?

3. When Paul refers to "principalities and powers" in Ephesians what is he referring to and why are they given this name?

4. Why was the inclusion of Gentiles in the Church such a controversial issue?

# Chapter One

**Key Points**

- God's purposes for us began in eternity and will finish in heaven.

- God's blessings include sanctification, adoption, redemption, forgiveness and the indwelling Spirit.

- God is in control no matter how chaotic things may seem.

- Christ has been raised from the dead and exalted above every rank of angel. The power that accomplished this is available to us.

Summarising Ephesians chapter one is not easy. The truths it teaches are not simple to define or explain. One way of setting about the task of studying the chapter is to work out what it is not. It is not -

- Direction for everyday living. This is apparent when we contrast it with e.g. the final chapter of Ephesians. Ephesians chapter six is rooted in the present and focussed on the concerns of everyday life. Ephesians chapter one spans eternity and is absorbed with positional and spiritual issues.
- Disputation with false teachers. Often when Paul writes he is seeking to answer questions or correct errors. Thus First Corinthians is largely composed of Paul's answers to questions the Corinthians had raised with him. But there is no trace of this in chapter one or for that matter the letter as a whole.
- Development of a doctrinal theme. In Romans he explains at length the relationship of the Law to the gospel

and the role of Israel now that the gospel was being preached to the Gentiles. There are themes in Ephesians, but they occur in subsequent chapters. Chapter one anticipates some of them but is not occupied with them.

What is the nature of the chapter then? It seems to me that chapter one is principally worship (vv. 3-14) and prayer (vv. 15-22).[22] While Christians still praise God and pray for His blessing, it is unusual for our praise and prayer to be committed to writing. In committing his worship and prayer to writing in this letter we get an insight into the heart and soul of the apostle. While instruction may not have been the primary purpose of these verses, they are rich in instruction.

**Our Praise**
The theme of praise is stated at the outset. Paul refers to the Ephesians' "spiritual blessings" (1:3). This gives us an immediate insight into the character of the chapter. Many blessings from God are physical and material. Israel was blessed with a Land and harvests and oftentimes deliverance from their enemies. But the blessings the Ephesians had received were "spiritual". In other words, they were not visible or tangible. While Israel undoubtedly had spiritual blessings the majority of them were physical. In contrast, the Church's blessings were spiritual. That said, the spiritual blessings of the present would become the tangible blessings of the future. Thus he writes to them about their sanctification and adoption as sons (1:4-5), their "redemption" and "forgiveness" (1:7). He also mentions their "inheritance" (1:11). The fullness of redemption and the appropriation of our inheritance is still future (1:14), but that does not mean that we do not have a present enjoyment of and entitlement to these blessings.

**Our Prayer**
In the prayer no one is mentioned by name. He does not refer to his imprisonment or pray for personal problems. He prays instead that they might have two key blessings - understanding and power. First of all, he deals with their need for understanding. His desire is that they might have "wisdom" and "revelation" or enlightenment (1:17). He prays that they might have "knowledge" and "understanding" (1:18). If

---

[22]Some of the material in ch 1 lies outside the boundaries of the worship and prayer e.g. his greeting (vv1,2) and a brief reference to their spiritual state (1:15).

the Ephesians truly understood what their "hope" was (1:18), other matters that troubled them would fall into perspective. If they had a deeper personal knowledge of the Lord Jesus, their lives would be different. If they understood the glory that awaited them when they received their inheritance that would be a preservative against many false hopes and aspirations here on earth.  So we can see that while specific prayer is a good thing since it requires us to say exactly what we feel and state exactly what we need, general prayers are equally vital.  If the apostle's prayers were answered the lives of the saints would have been transformed and prayers born of failure and misunderstanding would never need to be uttered.

## Our Power
God's power is an amazing thing (1:19). It created the universe. It holds all things together. But most amazing of all, it raised the Lord Jesus from the dead.  Now while God's power to impart life is well attested in Scripture, this was a different case.  In raising up Christ, God was defying the power of the devil. He not only restored the Lord's human life, but He supplied a new glorified existence.  He not only placed Him back on the earth, but He raised Him up to heaven. The One who is now far above all "principality and power" i.e. all angelic beings (3:10; 6:12), is the head of the Church.  So we are linked to One who enjoys supreme authority and exercises mighty power.

## Our Prominence
We have noticed that the chapter speaks of our "spiritual blessings".  But the apostle goes on to add that these blessings are "in heavenly places" (1:3).  Does this mean that none of the blessings can be enjoyed until we get to heaven? I suggest that there is an element of truth in that. These blessings will be enjoyed to the fullest extent in heaven.  But these are still blessings we enjoy in the present (2:6). Paul writes as if God's purpose in taking the saints to heaven was already accomplished.  Thus what we will realise actually when we are raised to sit with Christ we can appropriate spiritually in the present. The other aspect of the verse is that the blessings are "in heavenly places" because they stem from there.  Thus although they may be enjoyed here on earth they come from Christ who is enthroned in heaven.

## Our Predestination
Paul tells the Ephesians that they have been "chosen" and "predestined". The choice

of the saints was made "before the foundation of the world" that is before the events described in Genesis 1:1 occurred. The word "predestine" likewise encapsulates the idea of a purpose that was formed beforehand which God will bring to pass. That purpose crystallised when the Ephesian Christians were "adopted" and entered the family of God. This focus on God's eternal purposes may be to show that God was not like the gods that the Ephesians had served before their conversion. Diana and the other gods of the Greek pantheon were capricious whereas, God has settled and immutable purposes that cannot be thwarted.

But what had God chosen them for?  The passage tells us that He chose them so that they would (one day) be "holy and without blame". The words "holy" and "without blame" refer to the same idea, first from a positive and then a negative standpoint.  The idea that believers are holy has already been mentioned at the start of the chapter where they are described as "saints" (1:1) or holy ones. The same phrase re-occurs in 5:27 when Paul writes of the presentation of the Church to Christ after the rapture.[23]  While no doubt part of the reason God chose the Ephesians was so that in their daily living they would exhibit a holy character, the words "in His sight" are used in a similar context in Colossians to refer to the day of presentation (Col. 1:22). This would suggest that personal holiness in the present is not in view.[24] Holiness (whether positional or practical) is an aspect and consequence of salvation. When God saved us we were "sanctified". If we had not been sanctified we would not have been saved (1 Cor. 1:2; 6:11). Adoption as sons takes place on salvation and like sanctification is a feature of salvation (Rom. 8:15; Gal. 4:5).  Paul never seeks to explain how God's choice and predestination of the believer can be reconciled with the personal faith of the believer in God.  As the latter part of the chapter shows, Paul is very clear that no one is saved without personal trust in Christ (1:12, 13, 15, 19). While some have sought to say that they could not believe if God had not first chosen and predestined them, that is to go farther than Scripture states. Nowhere is God's choice said to be a precondition of human choice. Equally God's choice is never said to depend on man's choice. How it can be that divine choice and personal choice are simultaneously true is a matter that must be left to God.

---

[23]"holy and without blemish" is the same as "holy and without blame" in the original text.
[24]The parallel wording in Colossians is persuasive because Colossians was written contemporaneously with Ephesians and may therefore be thought to be a good guide to meaning. In Jude 24 κατενώπιον refers to our ultimate presentation to Christ in God's presence. By contrast "before" or "in the sight of" in 2 Cor 2:17 refers to our daily walk.

## Our Place

Sometimes as Christians we "don't know our place". We are inclined to think that we have a hold on God and that He must do as we ask. We sometimes look at Him through resentful eyes when things do not go as we would wish. The chapter refers to God's will on a number of occasions and shows that His will is paramount and that our will should be submissive to His. His will expressed itself in the appointment of Paul to apostleship (1:1) and the appointment of believers to holiness and sonship (1:3, 4) as well as an inheritance (1:11). God's will is not capricious or arbitrary but kind (1:9). Nothing is outside His will (1:11) – He "worketh all things after the counsel of His own will". He may conceal His will however and then reveal it at the time of His choosing (1:9). Thus, whatever we make of God's choices, we can never charge God with being unfair or heartless. His will is actuated by His grace (1:6). Grace is that divine quality that gives us what we do not deserve in contrast to mercy that withholds what we do deserve.

 KEY SCRIPTURES

Blessed *be* the God and Father of our Lord Jesus Christ, who hath blessed us with all spiritual blessings in heavenly *places* in Christ:

**Eph 1:3**

In whom we have redemption through his blood, the forgiveness of sins, according to the riches of his grace;

**Eph 1:7**

In whom ye also *trusted*, after that ye heard the word of truth, the gospel of your salvation: in whom also after that ye believed, ye were sealed with that holy Spirit of promise,

**Eph. 1:13**

that ye may know what is the hope of his calling, and what the riches of the glory of his inheritance in the saints, [19] And what *is* the exceeding greatness of his power to us-ward who believe,

**Eph. 1:18-19**

KEY QUOTES

The "heavenly realm" is the realm to which Christ has been raised (v. 20) and to which His people, united to Him by faith, have been raised with Him (Eph. 2:6). Even if they live on earth in mortal bodies, they can enter into the good of their heavenly inheritance here and now through the ministry of the Spirit (vv. 13-14). [25]

**F F Bruce**

In English the noun *sovereign* refers to "a person who possesses sovereign authority or power;" "a monarch or ruler." Human rulers, however, cannot exercise their authority absolutely because of finite limitations such as their mortality, fragile health, and limited knowledge. God does not have these limitations. He is infinite and thus His rule is one of absolute supremacy over all things under His control, namely the entire created realm. Not only, therefore, does God's sovereignty mean His "rule and authority over all things," but it means that He exercises this rule in accord with His own nature and decrees. Thus, being neither dependent nor limited in any way by anything outside Himself, God rules absolutely.[26]

**Robert V. McCabe**

[25] *The New International Commentary on the New Testament - The Epistle to the Colossians, to Philemon, and to the Ephesians* (Eerdmans) p.253.
[26] An Old Testament Sanctifying Influence: The Sovereignty of God. *Detroit Baptist Seminary Journal Volume* vol. 15 p.4.

## KEY QUESTIONS

1. How could God choose certain people to receive blessing before they were born or the world was created?

2. What sort of things does the chapter say God destined Christians to receive?

3. How can Christians living on earth be blessed in "the heavenlies"?

4. What sort of power does the Christian receive from God and why does he need it?

# Chapter Two

**Key Points**

- Salvation is the difference between life and death.

- Salvation is sourced in the love of God and expressed in mercy and grace.

- Salvation is for all people without distinction of race.

- The Church is one body: diverse yet united.

## A Regenerated People

The first section of chapter two (vv. 1-9) contains the apostle's teaching about salvation. Unlike chapter one where he is engaged in praise and prayer and where a reader learns by "listening in" to the apostle; here the apostle is speaking directly to the reader. While chapter one focuses primarily on the blessings that flow from salvation, here the apostle concentrates on salvation itself. He contrasts the state of the unsaved with that of the saved. It is interesting to note that in an epistle which has much to say about the power and influence of angels, he ascribes the state of the unsaved to the devil whom he describes as a "prince" and a "spirit". Though they may not appreciate it the unsaved are under the domination of the devil.

The apostle describes the way in which salvation is received. He points out that without the love of God and His mercy and grace it would be impossible (v4-5). On our part there must be a response to His love.  Faith is the condition placed by God on the reception of salvation. Why is the apostle teaching them this? The Ephesians were not Jews who had to be weaned away from the idea that their good works would procure salvation. It may be that Paul is teaching them that salvation comes from a God who is unlike the cruel and capricious gods of pagan mythology. In the beginning He created mankind but because of sin they died (Gen. 2:17). This was a spiritual as well as physical death. Rather than being God's children, mankind became the "children of disobedience". Now through salvation He is making man again (v10) so that they might live again and enjoy the fellowship that Adam forfeited.  Although the full realisation of life, resurrection and ascension remain future, Christians are in some measure in the good of this new life here and now (v5).

## A Reconciled People

Although the Jew and Gentile divide is not a major issue for us, it was a major issue for the apostle.  The early church was predominantly Jewish and a lot of the early Christians struggled to accept Gentiles. Paul himself was a Jew and the idea that Jew and Gentile should be united was not what he had been reared to believe.  His teaching in Ephesians is not directed at reluctant Jews but uncomprehending Gentiles. He wishes them to appreciate the enormity of the change accomplished in the gospel.  God had hitherto directed His blessings to the nation of Israel but now He had embraced the whole world (v12-13).  He speaks of this as equivalent to the knocking down of a wall.  A wall divides and God had removed the cause of division.  There was much that divided a Jew from a Gentile. In context it seems likely that the wall represents the ceremonial law (v15) since it excluded Gentiles and asked them to submit to customs which they would have found alien.

Paul's case for the inclusion of Jew and Gentile alike in one new entity called the Church begins with the cross. The inclusion of Jew and Gentile is because of the "blood of Christ".  Why the death of Christ required the union of Jew and Gentile is not specified.  The implication may be that it is unthinkable that the sacrificial death of God's Son should be limited to one nation or that the ceremony of the law should continue after the final sacrifice for sin. He also relies on the Lord's own message of reconciliation and unity (v17). The Lord Jesus had reached out to Gentiles whether it the Samaritans (Jn. 4:1-30) (relatives of the Jew) or complete strangers such as the Gentile centurion (Lk. 7:1-10) or the Canaanite woman (Matt. 15:21-28). What Paul now does is to continue the message preached by Christ and extend forgiveness to all through the death and resurrection of the Lord Jesus.

## A Reunited People

Prior to the giving of the Law there is no indication that any nation or person had preferential status in God's eyes. That changed when the sons of Jacob were chosen for blessing. The Covenant of Law entered at Sinai bound Israel to the Lord as His own people. The Gentiles, all non-Jewish people, lay outside this covenant. The nation of Israel proved that no matter how much privilege they enjoyed, man was still unable to obey God. Hence Law was superseded by grace. God reunited the Jew and Gentile through the cross. In the Church God is combining people of all nations. Paul describes this new body in a number of ways. A "man" (v15), a society (v19), a "household" (v19) and a "temple" (v20). Each of these metaphors underlines the unity of the Church. A body may have many members but it is united. A society may have many citizens but it is one group. A household may compose of a variety of people but they are one family. A temple may have many chambers and courts but it is one building. That said not all members of the Church are the same without differentiation. The temple has one keystone and a finite number of foundation stones. It has one Saviour, the Lord Jesus Christ, who is the founder of the Church. Contrary to the claims of the Roman Catholic Church and many other denominations there is no apostolic succession or prophetic continuity. The apostles and prophets were

## KEY SCRIPTURES

But God, who is rich in mercy, for his great love wherewith he loved us, [5] Even when we were dead in sins, hath quickened us together with Christ, (by grace ye are saved;).

**Eph 2:4-5**

**KEY SCRIPTURES**

But now in Christ Jesus ye who sometimes were far off are made nigh by the blood of Christ.

**Eph 2:13**

Now therefore ye are no more strangers and foreigners, but fellowcitizens with the saints, and of the household of God; [20] And are built upon the foundation of the apostles and prophets, Jesus Christ himself being the chief corner *stone;*

**Eph. 2:19-20**

## KEY QUOTES

First, he asserts that the salvation of the Ephesians was entirely the work, the free work, of God; but they had obtained this grace by faith. On one side, we must look at God; and, on the other, at men. God declares that He owes us nothing; so that salvation is not a reward or recompense, but mere grace. Now it may be asked how men receive the salvation offered to them by the hand of God? I reply, by faith. Hence he concludes that here is nothing of our own. If, on the part of God, it is grace alone, and if we bring nothing but faith, which strips us of all praise, it follows that salvation is not of us.[27]

**John Calvin**

Salvation is the gift of God from beginning to end, from planning to accomplishment. When Paul says it is "not of works" (2:9), he is giving a further elaboration of "not of yourselves" (v. 8). Not even deeds of righteousness can effect salvation. There can never be the slightest reason for man's personal glorying. Faith is the very opposite of works, for it offers no works to God but rather accepts that work of redemption that God has done. Thus Paul wrote in Romans 3:27 that God's plan of providing salvation through faith excludes all human boasting, for man has contributed nothing to it. Because fallen human nature is so prone to boast of its accomplishments and to take credit where there is even the slightest occasion, God devised a plan to save men in their hopelessness which allows no grounds whatever for human pride to operate.[28]

**Homer Kent**

[27]Commentary on the Epistle to the Ephesians.
[28]*Ephesians: The glory of the church* (Moody Press) p.39.

## ?? KEY QUESTIONS

1. What condition does God lay down as necessary on our part for salvation?

2. What inspired the plan of salvation?

3. When Paul spoke of a "wall" that divided Jews from Gentiles what was he speaking about?

4. What pictures does Paul use in Ephesians ch 2 to describe the Church?

# Chapter Three

**Key Points**

- The union of Jew and Gentile in the Church was a mystery hidden in the O.T. but revealed in the New Testament

- The opportunity to spread the gospel is a privilege as well as a duty.

- The Church is a display of God's wisdom in that it unites people who would otherwise be incompatible with one another.

- The dimensions of Christ's love for the Church are beyond human comprehension.

## The Miracle of the Gospel

The imprisonment that Paul refers to in v1 began when Paul was arrested by the Romans. He was arrested in an earthly temple (Acts 21:28, 33) because of his desire to create a spiritual temple (2:21). Even though preaching this message of forgiveness and reconciliation brought him great hardship, he saw the task as a privilege as well as a responsibility (v2 and 7). This did not "turn his head". Although he was prodigiously gifted and unflagging in his zeal, he still felt "less than the least of all saints" (v8). This sense of unworthiness may have been due in part to the fact that he had once persecuted Christians. To preach the gospel to Gentiles was a small way of showing his appreciation for the grace shown to him (v7).

## The Mystery of the Gospel

The idea that Jew and Gentile would be blessed on the same basis and have the same privileges (v6) was not taught in the O.T. (v5). Paul (Acts 9:15-16; 26:12-18) and Peter (Acts 10:9-

48) were given special revelations to convince them of this truth. This passage indicates that the other apostles received similar revelation (v5). Paul stresses that it was not a change of mind by God. The aim of uniting Jew and Gentile was conceived in eternity (v11). A truth not mentioned in the O.T. but revealed in the New Testament is often called a "mystery". There are a number of mystery doctrines.[29] Verses 3, 4 and 9 apply the term to the union of Jew and Gentile. Verse 9 in particular is a good example of how the term is used. It is a "mystery" not because it is not understood but because it was formerly unknown. Thus although the doctrine is now comprehensible it was previously a mystery.

## The Magnificence of the Gospel

There is also a heavenly dimension to the message. Paul teaches that angels learn from the Church (v10) the "manifold wisdom of God". The idea seems to be that God's wisdom can express itself in many different ways. In context this suggests that the enormous diversity of people that would form the Church would not be its downfall but would actually display God's wisdom. Angels who perhaps were not acquaint with the idea that God's glory could be promoted by people from a variety of races, nations and backgrounds would learn that God is glorified in the diversity of the Church. Unlike Israel the Church was varied in its composition. That such a union was possible declared the wisdom of God.

## The Measurements of the Gospel

The chapter closes with prayer and praise. His prayer is that they might be energised by the power of the Spirit and comforted by the presence of Christ. Usually emphasis is laid on the truth of the indwelling Spirit but here Paul speaks of the indwelling Christ. "Dwelling" is the opposite of visiting. Dwelling involves permanent residence. Paul's desire is that Christ should be a resident in the lives of the Ephesians not a mere visitor. His prayer ends with some of the most famous words ever penned by the apostle. He desires that they might know the "unknowable" (v19), the love of Christ. In other words he prays that the Ephesians might have an appreciation of something they would never fully understand. In order to make this point the apostle refers to the love of Christ in 4D. Most things have three dimensions – length, breadth and height. But he adds a fourth – depth. This stresses the supernatural love of the Lord Jesus. His

---

[29] e.g. the mystery of the resurrection of the church - 1 Cor. 15:51; the mystery of the deity and humanity of Christ - 1 Tim. 3:16.

desire is not merely that they should be in awe of that love but that it might have a stabilising influence on them (v17).  He closes by directing praise to God and desiring that the Church of which he has spoken might bring glory to God the Father not only in the present age but in all ages to come.

 ## KEY SCRIPTURES

> Unto me, who am less than the least of all saints, is this grace given, that I should preach among the Gentiles the unsearchable riches of Christ;
>
> **Eph 3:8**

> ...now unto the principalities and powers in heavenly *places* might be known by the church the manifold wisdom of God
>
> **Eph. 3:10**

> ...to comprehend with all saints what *is* the breadth, and length, and depth, and height; <sup>19</sup> And to know the love of Christ, which passeth knowledge, that ye might be filled with all the fulness of God.
>
> **Eph 3:18-19**

## KEY QUOTES

The love of Christ in its sweetness, its fulness, its greatness, its faithfulness, passeth all human comprehension. Where shall language be found which shall describe His matchless, His unparalleled love towards the children of men? It is so vast and boundless that, as the swallow but skimmeth the water, and diveth not into its depths, so all descriptive words but touch the surface, while depths immeasurable lie beneath. .. When He was enthroned in the highest heavens He was very God of very God; by Him were the heavens made, and all the hosts thereof. ... Who can tell His height of glory then? And who, on the other hand, can tell how low He descended? To be a man was something, to be a man of sorrows was far more; to bleed, and die, and suffer, these were much for Him who was the Son of God; but to suffer such unparalleled agony—to endure a death of shame and desertion by His Father, this is a depth of condescending love which the most inspired mind must utterly fail to fathom. Herein is love! and truly it is love that "passeth knowledge." [30]

**CH Spurgeon**

God had a secret hid in His heart ... He was erecting a stage upon which in our day He would introduce the church and display in it to these same angelic beings His very varied wisdom. If Jew and Gentile failed God in everything entrusted to them, and the climax of their guilt was seen in their joint condemnation to crucifixion of the Son of God, what an object lesson to angelic beings of the multifarious wisdom of God must be seen in Jew and Gentile joint-heirs, a joint-body and joint-partakers of God's promise. Here is the master-piece of divine wisdom.[31]

**Albert Leckie**

[30]*Morning and Evening* 28 March.
[31]*What the Bible teaches - Galatians, Ephesians, Philippians, Colossians, Philemon*, (John Ritchie Ltd), p. 129.

## ??? KEY QUESTIONS

1. When Paul describes the Church as a "mystery" what did he mean?

2. In what way can Christ live in our lives?

3. In what way is God's wisdom varied or multi-faceted?

4. What are the four dimensions of the love of Christ?

# Chapter Four

**Key Points**

- Christians should seek to live in unity.

- Unity is built on shared beliefs and blessings.

- In order to help Christians progress spiritually God has provided gifted men whose ministry is intended to bless the whole Church.

- Christians should be honest and upright in all that they do.

## The Church – its defining beliefs

Ephesians chapter 4 is the bridge between the doctrinal part of the letter (ch. 1-3) and the practical part of the letter. Verses 1-16 are largely doctrinal whereas vv.17-32 are largely practical.

Paul appreciated that it is difficult to unite people who are from different backgrounds. In Ephesus the Christians were largely Greeks who had been converted from paganism. But the churches were predominantly Jewish at that time. Tensions were inevitable not only within churches composed of Jew and Gentile but between churches of diverse backgrounds. He knew that the Jewish believers would find it hard to get over their disdain for people from pagan cultures. They had been reared to believe that they were superior to other peoples because of God's choice of Israel and the promises God had given Israel. Greeks on the other hand were proud of Greek culture and learning. Their language was read and spoken throughout the world and came to be the language of the New Testament. They would find it hard to co-operate with people who had a superiority complex since they had one as well!

Paul therefore encourages the Ephesians to be patient with one another (vv 2-3) and to focus on what they had in common (vv3-6). Paul lists a number of truths they could unite around. These are arranged in triplets.

**One Body -** God had united all Christians.  This idea is expressed in the picture of a body.  Although a body has many parts, the parts together make one body. In Ephesians the "body" is a figure of speech for all Christians e.g. 1:23; 4:12 and 16. Elsewhere the body is a metaphor for a company of Christians in a specific location (1 Cor. 12:27). Here he is focussed on the bigger picture.  He is teaching that all Christians form part of one universal church.  The negative aspect of this truth is that the Ephesians should no longer view themselves as part of the religious groups to which they formerly belonged.

**One Spirit** – it is interesting that, even when he is trying to focus on unity, Paul does not seek to focus on one God (Deut. 6:4; "the Shema"). Instead he focuses on the trinity.  Three persons united in one.  The first person is the Spirit. The Spirit is mentioned before the Lord Jesus and the Father in keeping with the idea that in the Church age, the Spirit is prominent. He has taken on the role occupied by Christ of unifying the disciples.  He may also have been pointing out that in contrast to the many gods of paganism and the evil spirits that lay behind them, there was one Spirit, the "Spirit of truth".

**One hope -** the hope arises from "the calling" of the Christians.  In the New Testament the "calling" of the Christian occurs at salvation (see v1 where "vocation" means calling).  Just as Jesus called the disciples from their old lives to follow Him so believers are called by God to serve Him. But specifically this refers to the hope of final salvation in our resurrection and final deliverance through the gospel. The Lord Jesus expressed the same idea when He said "I am the way, the truth and the life".  The only way to salvation is through the gospel.

**One Lord** – this refers to the second person of the godhead, the Lord Jesus.  The

Bible places this triplet of statements in verse 5.  Identifying Him as Lord rather than the Lord Jesus or as Christ is probably designed to draw attention to His authority as Lord. Hence Christians have only one master and own allegiance to no other.

**One faith** – sometimes the Bible refers to personal faith which is the faith of each believer.  Sometimes it speaks of the faith as a name for the body of doctrine which Christians accept.  It makes better sense to interpret this verse as a reference to the latter.  This is because there is only one faith i.e. one body of doctrine.  By contrast there are many faiths in the sense that there are many Christians who have faith. See as follows, "earnestly contend for the faith which was once delivered unto the saints" (Jude 3); "...in the latter times some shall depart from the faith" (1 Tim 4:1). Paul does not here specify what doctrines comprise "the faith".  Some passages indicate the scope of fundamental truth e.g. Hebrews 6:1b; Acts 2:41-42.

**One baptism –**  One baptism probably refers to the fact that for Christians there is only one type of baptism, which is in the name of the Lord Jesus and by immersion. There were other baptisms in New Testament times but only one that identified the believer with the Lord. While it may mean baptism in the Spirit, this truth would sit more comfortably in the preceding triplet which is linked with the Spirit.

**One God –** here is the last member of the godhead, the Father.  The structure here is different. He stands alone rather than being bracketed with other truths. Three of His attributes are identified. He is "above all" which refers to His pre-eminence, He is "through all" which refers to His power to achieve His ends through man, whether they aware of this or not, and "in you all" which refers to His presence in the believer.

The Ephesian epistle was written when, despite the efforts of the Judaisers, there was still a visible unity in the Church. The consensus of belief and practice that this depended upon gradually eroded.  Paul's later epistles show how the apostle dealt with the situation where the teaching of the apostles was rejected (1Tim. 6:3-5; 2 Tim. 2:16, 21, 23; 3:14; 4:2). A common belief in the Father, Son and Holy

Spirit; a common salvation and hope of heaven; a common baptism in the name of Jesus Christ and a common adherence to "the faith" is the foundation of unity between Christians.

## The Church – its diversity of gifts

The section from v7-17 shows that a united Church is also a diverse Church. The Lord Jesus is depicted, using words adapted from Psalm 68, as a victor who returns from battle with prisoners ("He led captivity captive") and hands out gifts as spoils of war to His people ("He gave gifts unto men"). The reference to "captives" is simply part of the image of a triumphant victor drawn from the Psalm and is not intended to suggest that the Lord actually took prisoners to heaven. The gifts are likened to the spiritual gifts Christ gave to the Church after His ascension. In Psalm 68 the capital city to which the victor returns is Jerusalem on Mount Zion. Paul draws the analogy with Christ returning to heaven. He makes the point that the One who ascended up "on high" (to heaven) is the One who first descended to earth. The expression the "lower parts of the earth" was interpreted by the Church fathers to mean the realm of the dead. Reading this passage with 1 Peter 3:19-20 they believed that the Lord Jesus after death went into hell and delivered the saints from their captivity ("the spirits in prison") and took them to heaven. A surprising amount of Bible teachers still follow this view. A simpler way of looking at the passage is to interpret "on high" and "the lower parts of the earth" as representing on the one hand a place of glorification and on the other as a place of humiliation. The Lord was born in humiliating circumstances in Bethlehem, He was reared in Nazareth a disreputable town and He was crucified at Calvary where criminals were executed. While the counterpart of heaven  might be thought to be hell, it is unthinkable that the Lord would be dispatched to a "prison" for the spirits of the dead after His sufferings on the cross. Moreover such a view contradicts His statement that after death He would go to "Paradise" (Lk. 23:43), an expression that describes heaven itself (2 Cor. 12:4). There is no indication He descended into the spirit world during the 40 days prior to the ascension, far less "upper hades" or "lower hades", expressions which do not appear in Scripture.

In other passages, gifts are described as miraculous endowments of the Spirit (1 Cor. 12:8). Here the gifts are identified with the men who God has gifted. The ambit of gift here is narrower than that in Romans 12:4-8 since it is confined to public gifts and those who exercised them.  Apostles, if the examples of Paul and Peter are anything to go by, possessed a variety of gifts and a leadership role over the whole Church.  Prophets were God's spokesmen and spoke directly for God to the people without requiring to read and interpret Scripture. Evangelists preached the gospel.  Pastors and teachers refer to one gift. He was a "pastor" or shepherd, as well as a teacher.  This combination of shepherd care mean they taught in a way that benefitted the people of God. In this section it is clear that these gifts are to the Church as a whole.  Thus while each is a member of a local church, their ministry was for the benefit of the whole Christian community.  The purpose behind these gifts is so that the Church might grow (4:12) until the day when God's purpose is complete and the Church is taken to heaven (4:13, 30). The ultimate maturity of the Church will be a work of God and will not depend on gift. Only then will the Church reach full maturity and each saint acquire a perfect knowledge of the Son of God. This will occur at the resurrection of the saints and rapture of the church. In the meanwhile He has given gifts to assist the Church reach its potential.

## The Church - its difference in lifestyle
From 4:17 onwards to the end of the letter Paul speaks about the practical issues of life. Christians should be different from society around them.  We do not party or strive after wealth (v19).  The "old man" with his tastes and behaviour should be "put off" just as an item of clothing is put off (v22).  We should strive to "put on the new man". In one sense this occurred on salvation (Col. 3:10) when in God's eyes the "old man" who was associated with Adam was put off and we "put on" the "new man" who is associated with Christ.  But in practical terms the old man is linked with our old nature which is still present within each believer. The flesh needs to be "put off".  Verse 25 describes the soiled clothing of lying, anger, dishonesty and bad language. This can be exchanged for the clean clothes of truthfulness, good temper, honesty and pure speech.  4:30 teaches that God is not indifferent to our behaviour. The Spirit is "grieved" when we sin. In conclusion he points out that we should not be "mouthy".  The angry and bitter language which belongs to the world should give way to behaviour which is kind, gentle and forgiving.

KEY SCRIPTURES

*There is* one body, and one Spirit, even as ye are called in one hope of your calling; [5] One Lord, one faith, one baptism, [6] One God and Father of all, who *is* above all, and through all, and in you all.

**Eph 4:4-5**

He gave some, apostles; and some, prophets; and some, evangelists; and some, pastors and teachers; [12] For the perfecting of the saints, for the work of the ministry, for the edifying of the body of Christ:

**Eph. 4:11-12**

And be ye kind one to another, tenderhearted, forgiving one another, even as God for Christ's sake hath forgiven you.

**Eph 4:32**

 KEY QUOTES

In essentials, unity; in non-essentials, liberty; in all things, charity.

**Rupertus Meldenius**

When Niccolo Paganini willed his finely crafted and lovingly used violin to the city of Genoa, he demanded that it never be played again. It was a gift designated for preservation, but not destined for service.

On the other hand, when the resurrected Christ willed His spiritual gifts to the children of God, He commanded that they be used. They were gifts not designated for preservation, but destined for service.

**Michael Green**

## KEY QUESTIONS

1. In what way does the Trinity illustrate the ideal of unity among the people of God?

2. What is "the faith"?

3. What does the expression "the lower parts of the earth" mean?

4. In what way are the sins of the flesh similar to items of clothing?

# Chapter Five

**Key Points**

- The Christian should be morally pure.

- The Christian's speech should be sober.

- The Christian should not be greedy.

- Christian marriage should be marked by fidelity and love

**Christian Mimicry**

The opening verses of ch. 5 are linked with the closing verse of ch. 4. In 4:32 the apostle has encouraged people to forgive one another as God has forgiven us. In ch 5:1 he encourages us to imitate God. Forgiving others, when we would not naturally be inclined to do so, involves imitating God. The Greek word translated "followers" is *mimetai* from which we get the word "mimic". Paul says we should be followers of God "as dear children". He knew that children copy their parents or those that they admire. So it should be with Christians. There is a saying that "imitation is the sincerest form of flattery". In other words people who are sincere in their admiration of others tend to copy their behaviour. We should copy God. That imitation covers other aspects of God's nature. Christ gave Himself sacrificially (5:2). So we ought to give sacrificially.

**Christian Morals**

The apostle then lists a series of

behaviours that are inconsistent with God's character. Sexual intimacy before marriage is forbidden. Sexual unfaithfulness after marriage is forbidden (v3). Greed is forbidden. Bad language is forbidden (v4). Empty chatter is forbidden. People whose lives are characterised by such behaviour will never enter God's kingdom[32] (v5). He is not saying that a Christian who commits these sins cannot enter the kingdom. Sadly, Christians do commit these sins. But he is assuming that no one who has been truly born again could possibly live a life characterised by these sins (see v 7). If someone who professed salvation did live such a life, then his profession would be empty. The kingdom spoken of here is a future kingdom since it will be "inherited". This presupposes that at some point in the future the saints will receive a kingdom as an inheritance.

It is interesting to note that Paul describes the covetous man as an "idolater" (v5). This does not mean that he actually worshipped an idol of stone or wood. Paul means that the person worshipped wealth rather than God. No doubt he did not worship gold or silver as such but accumulating wealth had displaced God as the main focus of his life. When that happens a person has become an idolater.

In the middle of the section (v8-14), Paul utilises language we usually associate with the apostle John. He speaks of "light" and "darkness". John and other Bible authors often link light with good and darkness with evil. Paul's point is that Christians should live upright lives. Paul intermixes this metaphor with another metaphor viz. fruitfulness, and links "light" with "fruit" (vv. 9 and 11). Fruitfulness speaks of that which is good and wholesome. Verse 14 is a quotation but it is not clear what is being quoted since there is no O.T. passage that follows these words. It may be a hymn expressing the idea that on salvation we rise from spiritual death and Christ shines on us as the sun shines on those who have emerged from darkness into the day.

It is obvious that Paul considered the pagan world in which the Ephesians lived as irredeemably corrupt. Some of their sins were so gross that it was a shame even to speak about them (v12). Roman and Greek society tolerated virtually any kind

---

[32]God's kingdom includes the idea of being taken to heaven which is a realm under His kingship but extends beyond that to the return of the Church to the new earth after the Millennium.

of sexual behaviour. Relations between persons of the same sex, with children and slaves were all considered acceptable. Many societies have begun to move back towards the moral standards of ancient Greece and Rome. More generally Paul warns the Ephesians against immorality between the sexes. These days those who refrain from sexual relations before marriage are unusual. Likewise spouses who remain faithful to their partners are sometimes the exception rather than the rule.

## Christian Moderation

Christians are also expected to be wise and exercise moderation in all they do. One key aspect of wisdom is the proper use of time. Time is a precious commodity. It can be frittered away or it can be "redeemed" (v16). In other words it can serve useful purposes or it can serve worldly purposes. In the O.T. if an object was redeemed it was transferred out of one person's ownership into the ownership of another by the payment of a redemption price. The apostle encourages us to "buy back" time so that it is utilised for proper purposes. Paul's warning against drunkenness is a warning that time spent drinking is wasted time (v18).

## Christian Melody

By contrast he gives an example of a profitable use of time and refers to hymn singing. Hymns travel horizontally (v19) and vertically (v20). The words and music combine to bless those who engage in the singing. It seems clear from the fact that the singers "speak" to one another that corporate hymn singing is in view. These are not solos. The hymns also involve praise to God as we "give thanks". The melody arises from the heart which stresses the idea that God is not so much interested in the tunefulness of the voice or the musical arrangement as the delight the singer takes in the subject of praise.

## Christian Marriage

The final section of ch. 5 focuses on the relationship between a wife and a husband. Paul deals with the woman first and teaches that a wife should submit to her husband. Since marriage is a partnership between two people, couples often have to make decisions about matters affecting them both. This passage teaches that a wife cannot disregard her husband's wishes or seek to impose her wishes in preference to her husband's. Submission involves deference to the husband. The passage does not entitle the husband to operate as a sort of dictator. As we will see, his obligation of love to her forbids that. In a successful marriage decisions are made with a bit of "give and take". A wife should be completely free to express her point of view. But ultimately where there is a difference of opinion, the wife should submit. She should do so in good grace and not conduct a form of "guerrilla warfare" against her husband as retaliation!

Next, Paul deals with men and teaches that a husband is expected to love his wife. The obligation of love is different from the obligation of submission. Love may inspire a great variety of behaviours whereas submission is a particular attitude. Submission may arise from love, obedience or passivity. The standard set for the husband's love is Christ's love for the Church. His love was sacrificial and unqualified so a very high standard is set. It is noteworthy that Paul does not teach that a wife should love her husband. He might have done so since mutual love, unlike mutual submission, is both possible and desirable. In focussing on the husband's obligation to love he may be signalling that callousness and indifference is primarily a male affliction. He is assuming that a woman who is loved will love in return.

There is no indication that the obligations mentioned in this section depend on the worthiness of the other party. We might expect a wife to be relieved of her obligation of submission if the husband is unpleasant. We might expect the husband to be relieved of his obligation of love if the wife is unfaithful. Subject to the qualification below, this is not the apostle's teaching. The duties of submission and love arise not because the other party deserves it but because the Lord requires them and the relationship of marriage flourishes if nurtured by them. The reason why the Church submits to Christ is that He created it and it owes its existence to Him. Similarly (although this is implied) the wife stands in the position of Eve as one who derives her existence from Adam and was made to be a support to Adam. Likewise men should love their wives not only because God wishes them to but because it is the proper thing to do.

Are the obligations of submission and love unqualified? If the wife finds herself with a husband who beats or abuses her, her obligation of submission does not compel her to adhere (see 1 Cor. 7:15).[33] If a wife deserts her husband or is unfaithful to him he should still seek to love her no matter how unworthy of that love she has proved to be.  Christ loved the church although it has proved to be unfaithful and disobedient and His love is our measure. [34]

## KEY SCRIPTURES

Be ye therefore imitators of God, as beloved children, (J.N.D.)

**Eph 5:1**

And be not drunk with wine, wherein is excess; but be filled with the Spirit;

**Eph. 5:18**

Wives, submit yourselves unto your own husbands, as unto the Lord.

**Eph 5:22**

Husbands, love your wives, even as Christ also loved the church, and gave himself for it.

**Eph 5:25**

---

[33]This verse does not teach that a person who is badly treated and who flees an abusive relationship is free to remarry (see 1 Cor. 7:11). While one of the key accompaniments of marriage is  the obligation to adhere or co-habit if someone refuses to live with their marriage partner this is called desertion. In 1 Cor. 7:11 Paul teaches that if one of the marriage partners refuses to live with the other, there is nothing that can be done about that. Thus a Christian lady whose partner has left her and will not live with her need not constantly seek re-union. That would only bring constant disruption and heartache when "God has called us to peace" (1 Cor. 7:15) . But the passage does not mean that desertion is a basis for terminating the marriage bond. The broad theme of the chapter is that parties should accept the status quo (1 Cor. 7:20, 24).  Thus the wife should accept that while her marriage is for practical purposes over she is not at liberty to see it as dissolved in God's eyes and seek a new partner (1 Cor 7:10-11, 39).
[34]Some argue that the "fornication" of Matt. 5:32 and 19:9 is (or includes) adultery and that there is permission to remarry where adultery occurs. Others consider that "fornication" means pre-marital intercourse. In my view this is the correct interpretation. Engagements (called betrothal in those days) according to the practice of the Jews required to be terminated by divorce (Lk. 2:5; Matt. 1:18, 19) so there was a sensible reason in the Lord's day for ending betrothal where there had ben pre-marital sin. While fornication (porneia) can cover sexual sins including adultery (1 Cor. 6:13; Eph 5:3) the context sometimes shows that it has a narrow meaning viz. premarital intercourse; e.g. Jn 8:41. Adultery (moichao) has only one meaning i.e. intercourse outside the marriage bond . Where both words are used side by side I consider the purpose is to contrast fornication with adultery. As regards Matt 5:32 and 19:9 It would be odd if the Lord condemned sex outside marriage as adultery and then permitted the wrongdoer in reliance on his or her sin to divorce. Those who consider that the Lord permits divorce on the grounds of adultery often acknowledge that this would be anomalous. To deal with the problem some suggest that a divorce on the grounds of fornication (i.e. adultery) is available only to the innocent party. However the Lord says nothing about that. Anyone with practical experience of marriage counselling will tell you that it is often impossible to allocate blame. Adultery is often the symptom not the cause of breakdown.

## KEY QUOTES

Even if marriages are made in heaven, humans have to be responsible for their maintenance.

To forgive is not for personal gain, nor indeed primarily for the good of others, but something that is done for God and the result is pleasurable to Him.

**Albert Leckie**

A young minister was to perform his first wedding ceremony. Fearing he might forget something, he sought counsel from an older minister. The experienced man told the young minister everything he needed to do and made one final suggestion: "If you ever forget what you are supposed to say, just quote Scripture."

The ceremony went smoothly until he pronounced the happy couple husband and wife. At that point, his mind went blank. That's when he remembered the advice of the old preacher to quote Scripture. So he quoted the only verse that came to his mind: "Father, forgive them, for they know not what they do."

## KEY QUESTIONS

1. In what way is greed like idolatry?

2. In what way can time be redeemed?

3. Why do Christians sing hymns?

4. What are the implications of a husband being obliged to love his wife in the same way as Christ loved the Church?

# Chapter Six

**Key Points**

- Christian children should obey their parents.

- Christian employees should be good workers.

- Christian employers should treat their staff fairly.

- God has provided Christians with all the resources they need to face a hostile world.

## CHILDREN AND PARENTS

The opening paragraphs of Ephesians ch. 6 continue to deal with relationships in the home. In this section Paul deals with children and their parents and slaves and their masters.

Paul highlights two overlapping obligations children owe to their parents. These are the obligations of obedience and honour. The obligation of obedience arises because the Bible teaches that parents have authority over their children until they become independent (see e.g. Eph 5:21). The obligation to honour parents is a wider duty and continues for as long as the parent lives (1 Tim 5:8). That such an obligation was expressed in the Ten Commandments shows how fundamental the issue is.

There are obvious reasons why a child should obey his or her parents. Children lack the maturity to know what is good for them – though they may not see that. Children also tend to focus on their own needs whereas adults are more inclined and better equipped to take account of collective interests, such as that of the family. The Lord Jesus was submissive to Joseph and Mary (Lk. 2:51) even though at times their wishes were contrary to His. Children should seek to follow His example. Honour is rooted in different considerations. Honour is based on the respect that a child should have for parents as opposed to the authority parents wield. Respect is based on an acknowledgement that the child owes its existence to parents and the sacrifices parents make in order to rear children (cp. Heb. 12:9).

Does this passage mean children must obey their parents in all circumstances? The answer strictly speaking is "no". Thus for example if a parent wishes a child to tell a lie or act unlawfully, obedience would be wrong. In general however obedience is the rule. The family as an institution goes back to creation and may be seen in various guises across all cultures. The obligations set out by Paul describe a natural order. If so the obligations of obedience and honour describe what is proper and do not does not depend on whether the parents or children for that matter are Christian or not. Nor do they depend on whether the parents are in the eyes of the child "good" parents.

Everyone would acknowledge that children mature at different rates. Most agree however that childhood is left behind by the mid to late teens. Thus for example a girl can consent to be married when she is 16. A boy can drive a car when he is 17. These factors suggest that society considers that a child can be trusted to make important decisions for themselves and undertake responsibility by their late teens.

## MASTERS AND SLAVES

Although slavery is unknown now in the UK, slavery was lawful in the Roman Empire of which the city of Ephesus was part. Indeed slavery was common throughout the world at that time and was permitted under O.T. law. In the New Testament slaves were part of everyday life and were found in most households. The abolition of slavery has not made Paul's teaching redundant. Although the fit between the master-servant relationship and the employee-employer relationship is not a neat one, the principles that Paul sets out cross the boundaries between slavery and employment.

The main lessons are that Christians should be obedient to their Employer and that their service should be whole hearted. They should not do the minimum necessary to get by. The Christians' standard is that which they would offer to Christ. Of course Christians should not as far as possible allow their employment to get in the way of other aspects of their service for Christ such as gathering with the assembly.

In light of all this, Christian employees need to be wary about opposing their employers in disputes over pay and conditions. There is no harm in standing up for what is fair and just but the Christian cannot confront his employer. It is admitted that the employer-employee relationship is more complex than the master-slave relationship. The masters in Ephesus are today multinational corporations with Human Resources departments and detailed employment policies intended to protect the employees from exploitation. But sometimes pay disputes can be power struggles between two sides determined to get the best possible deal. Trade Union membership can also be problematic. While not all Trade Unions are militant, some support causes that are hard to reconcile with Scripture.

The masters are obliged to "do the same things unto them" i.e. the slaves (6:9). In other words, Paul teaches that masters have to treat their slaves with the same respect and sincerity of heart they would show to Christ. Although Paul never advocated the abolition of slavery, these words fatally undermine all the exploitative aspects of slavery as well as the institution itself. The idea of "owning" another human being as one might own a tool or animal is incompatible with Paul's teaching. Thus although Paul did not say anything which could have been understood as a political or revolutionary ambition (about one third of the Roman Empire were in slavery and its economy depended on them) he taught principles that would, if practised, lead to its abolition.

## CHRISTIANS AND THE DEVIL

The epistle closes with a picture of the "Christian soldier". In Ephesians the Christian's adversary is not so much the world or the flesh but the devil. The world is under the control of the devil (Eph. 2:2) not Prime Ministers or Emperors. Even the "air" surrounding the earth is populated by evil powers (Eph. 2:2). To meet this foe God supplies him with weapons and armour with which to defend himself.  The armour must however be "put on" (Eph 6:11; 13).  It is no good languishing in the locker!  Hence protection is found in the measure we are in the good of the provision God has made.  Paul is not suggesting that the armour is used every day or that the Devil is constantly attacking. But every now and then an "evil day" arrives (6:13).  In that "evil day" the attacks are energised by the devil and implemented by his emissaries ("principalities", "powers" and "rulers"). He does not specify what form the attack may take and he does not insist that every trial or difficulty is energised by Satan. But he does insist that to ward off these attacks the Christian needs to be in the good of "truth", "righteousness", "the gospel", "faith", "salvation" and the "word of God".  These defences interlink like mail. The "word of God" is the source of "truth". "Salvation" is the product of the "gospel". "Righteousness" comes through "faith". While the metaphor may be inspired by O.T. depictions of the Lord as a warrior it is more likely that it refers to the equipment of the Roman soldiers that formed part of Paul's daily life in Rome when he wrote this letter. Each had a belt round his waist which "girded their loins". From it hung the scabbard for the sword and kept his tunic in place. They wore a breastplate and sturdy marching shoes.  They carried shields, wore a helmet and bore a sword.  These six items are supplemented by a further "defence" - watchfulness (6:18).  If a soldier sleeps, his enemies may overpower him no matter how fine his armour.  While the picture is largely one of defence, the Christian may carry the battle to the opposition; hence the reference to the gospel as depicted by a soldier's footwear.  With such shoes he may "stand firm" (6:11, 13) and "wrestle" (6:12) in close combat but also march forward with the message (6:15, 19). The sword is both an offensive as well as defensive weapon. The only items of a legionary's equipment that are omitted in this metaphor are the spear and leg guards ("greaves").

## KEY SCRIPTURES

Children, obey your parents in the Lord: for this is right.

**Eph. 6:1**

Servants, be obedient to them that are *your* masters.

**Eph. 6:5**

Put on the whole armour of God, that ye may be able to stand against the wiles of the devil.

**Eph. 6:11**

Praying at all times in the Spirit, with all prayer and supplication.

**Eph 6:18 9 (E.S.V.)**

## KEY QUOTES

Obedience is required of the child. The Preacher Solomon said, 'Woe to thee, O land when thy king is a child', Eccl. 10. 16. He acknowledged that the child's lot was to obey, not to be obeyed. If that child has trusted the Lord, that obedience is to be 'in the Lord', Eph. 6. 1. What then is obeying 'in the Lord'? It is more than was demanded in the Old Testament, for it involves the recognition of the Lordship of Christ. Paul adds: 'this is right', so it is a question of righteousness. He also quotes the fifth commandment: 'honour thy father and mother'. Clearly, honouring parents is not just a case of outward acts; there must also be inward feelings, for honour is one of the ways love expresses itself. Paul adds one other feature of Christian obedience. Not only is it a question of righteousness and of love; it is also the 'first commandment with promise', Eph. 6. 2.[35]

**Tom Wilson**

[35]Precious Seed 2008 Issue 63.

## KEY QUOTES

Before engaging an enemy, it is wise to be acquainted with his nature besides his numerical and military strength. "We wrestle not against flesh and blood", indicating that our enemy is not human, "but against principalities, against powers", which means that he is super-human. .... In warfare, it is important to gain knowledge of the enemy's positions in the battlefield through reconnaissance. Whilst we are not told to reconnoitre enemy territory, we know that the location of our spiritual conflict is "in the heavenlies" R.V., which does not mean heaven, the dwelling-place of God. Satan is "the prince of the power of the air", 2. 2, and so the devil and his principalities and powers operate in the atmospheric heavens which are termed "the heavenlies" in the verse before us.  However, we must neither under-estimate the enemy nor resist him unarmed. For conflict with these "rulers of the darkness of this world", we need to put on "the armour of light", knowing that the enemy is fearful of the light, Rom. 13. 12. When faced with "the wicked one" and his "spirits of wickedness", we must wear "the armour of righteousness" for protection.[36]

**J D B Page**

---

[36]Precious Seed 1977 Issue 5.

## KEY QUESTIONS

1. What is the difference between a child who obeys its parents and a child that honours its parents?

2. What are the obligations of masters to slaves and do they have any parallels with the relationship between employers and employees today?

3. In what way is the Christian subject to attack by the devil?

4. What can a Christian do to protect himself against attack?

# INTRODUCTION TO THE LETTER TO THE COLOSSIANS

## Introduction
There are five letters in the New Testament that were written by Paul while in prison.  This is evident from the terms of the letters.  In Ephesians he refers to himself as the "prisoner of Jesus Christ" (Eph. 3:1; 4:1); in Colossians he speaks of a "fellow prisoner" called Aristarchus (Col. 4:10); in Philippians he refers to his "bonds" (Phil. 1:7, 13, 14 and 16) and in Philemon he refers to himself as "a prisoner of Jesus Christ" (Phm. 9).  In 2 Timothy there is also reference to an imprisonment (2 Tim 1:8, 16) but in view of the information about Paul's movements in the letter it is commonly agreed that this is a later imprisonment which culminated in his execution.  The Prison Epistles are usually linked to the imprisonment which began Acts 21:33 in Jerusalem and ends with Paul under house arrest in Rome (Acts 28:16, 30).

## Philemon and Colossians
In Colossians Paul refers to an Onesimus who was travelling to Colossae.  Paul describes him as "one of you" i.e. from Colossae (Col. 4:9). In his letter to Philemon he refers to an Onesimus who was a runaway slave (Phm 10-12) whom he was returning to Philemon. This link suggests that the two letters were written at the same time and that Philemon lived in Colossae and was part of the church there.

## Ephesians and Colossians
Both present Christ as a triumphant figure who has subdued all adversaries (Col. 2:15: Eph 1:20-22; 4:8). Both focus on salvation as a release from Satanic power (Col. 1:13, 21; Eph 2:3-4). Both focus on the union of Jew and Gentile in one body – the church (Col. 1:26: Eph 2:12-14; 3:6).  Both contain a section with detailed instruction for the home dealing, in the same order, with (a) husbands and wives (Eph 5:22-33; Col. 3:18-19), (b) children and parents (Eph 6:1-4; Col. 3:20-21) and (c) masters and servants (Eph. 6:5-9; Col. 4:1). In the closing greetings of the letters there are two passages (Eph. 6:21-22 and Col. 4:7-9) which are virtually identical

**Structure -** The opening section of both letters comprises of worship followed by prayer.  The prayers are stimulated by the apostle having heard of their faith and love (Eph 1:15; Col 1:3) and his desire that they will have a fuller understanding of God coupled with greater power in their service for Him (Col 1:4; Eph 1:17; Col 1:11; Eph 1:19).

**Style -** The letters are also written in a similar style. As Ephesians is characterised by lengthy sentences so is Colossians.  Chapter 1 has only five sentences, and one of these (vv. 9-20) is made up of 218 words.[37] The apostle not only used long sentences but when he seeks to express a thought he also multiplies words for effect. Thus e.g. in ch. 1 he might have prayed that the Colossians would know God's will. Instead he prays that they might be "filled with the knowledge of his will in all wisdom and spiritual understanding" (Col 1:9) an approach that adds layers of truth rather than making one basic point.  In ch 2 he might have prayed that the Colossians would "know God". Instead he prays that they might have "the full assurance of understanding, to the acknowledgement of the mystery of God" (Col. 2:2); cf. Eph. 1:17, 18.

**Phrases and ideas –** In Col. 1:13 he describes the Lord Jesus as "His dear Son". In Eph. 1:6 he describes Him as the "Beloved".  In Ephesians the Christian is presented as someone who has been already resurrected and taken to God's presence in the "heavenlies". Although Colossians does not use the word "heavenlies" it presents the Christian as resurrected (Col. 2:12) and ascended (Col 3:1).  Both speak of salvation as similar to putting on new clothes; see the phrase "putting off" and "putting on" (Col. 3:8, 10, 12, 14; Eph. 4:22, 24).  In both, there is reference to hymns. The apostle encourages them to sing with "grace in your hearts to the Lord" (Col 3:16) and make "melody in your heart to the Lord" (Eph. 5:19).  In both he describes a man who is covetous as an idolater (Eph. 5:5; Col 3:5) – quite an unusual turn of phrase.  In both he uses the word "fullness" in a way which is unique to these epistles.  Although the word fullness occurs elsewhere in Scripture to describe the full characteristics of deity, in Ephesians the Church is "the fullness of Him who fills all in all" (Eph. 1:22-23), Christians may be filled with the "fullness of God" (Eph. 3:19) and after the resurrection will acquire "the fullness of Christ" (Eph. 4:13). In Colossians "the fullness of God" dwelt in Christ (Col. 1:19; 2:9) and we have achieved completeness (lit. "fullness') in Christ (Col. 2:10). Both speak of the unsaved as "alienated" (Eph. 2:12; 4:18 and Col. 1:21), of the need to "redeem the time" (Eph. 5:16 and Col. 4:5) and of believers as "rooted" (Eph. 3:17 and Col. 2:7).  The gospel is "the word of truth, the gospel" (Eph. 1:13 and Col. 1:5).  Both use similar wording to describe the believers' links with Christ and one another e.g. "held together," "supply" (Eph.

---

[37]E.g. Col. 1:3-8, 9-20; 2:8-15; 3:5-11.

4:16 and Col. 2:19).  Col. 1:14 "in whom we have redemption through His blood, even the forgiveness of sin" and Eph. 1:7 "in whom we have redemption through His blood, the forgiveness of sins, according to the riches of His grace" are nearly identical.

## Differences
- Colossians is shorter than Ephesians.
- Colossians focuses on the person of Christ (Col. 1:15-19; 2:3, 9) as well as His work whereas Ephesians focuses on the work He has done.
- Colossians confronts and corrects erroneous doctrine see e.g. 2:8, 16, 20 unlike Ephesians which has no (explicitly) corrective element in it.
- Colossians has a long greetings section (Col. 4:7-17) whereas Ephesians does not convey any greetings.
- Colossians only mentions the Holy Spirit once (1:8) whereas Ephesians mentions the Spirit thirteen times.
- While Paul had been to Ephesus and had planted the church there, he had never been to Colossae (Col. 2:1).  He does not refer to individuals by name in Ephesians. Colossians by contrast has long list of people to whom he sends greetings in ch 4.
- In Colossians when Paul speaks of the church he refers to the local assembly, whereas in Ephesians the Church is the whole body of believers.

## The City of Colossae
Colossians was a city located about 100 miles east of Ephesus.   Unlike Ephesus it had no particular claim to fame. It was destroyed by an earthquake shortly after the letter to the Colossians was written and never rebuilt. Today, the ancient site lies in ruins with a modern town, Chronas, located nearby. Colossae is not mentioned elsewhere in Scripture and it seems Paul had never met the people to whom he wrote (2:1). The gospel may have been brought there by Timothy (1:1) or Epaphras (1:7).

## An Outline of Colossians
   I.  Doctrine: Christ's Preeminence Declared (1)
       A. In the Gospel message (1:1–12)
       B. In the cross (1:13–14)

    C. In creation (1:15–17)
    D. In the church (1:18–23)
    E. In Paul's ministry (1:24–29)
II.  Danger: Christ's Preeminence Defended (2)
    A. Beware of empty philosophies (2:1–10)
    B. Beware of religious legalism (2:11–17)
    C. Beware of man-made discipline and asceticism (2:18–23)
III. Duty: Christ's Preeminence Displayed (3–4)
    A. In personal purity (3:1–11)
    B. In Christian fellowship (3:12–17)
    C. In the home (3:18–21)
    D. In daily work (3:22–4:1)
    E. In Christian witness (4:2–6)
    F. In Christian service (4:7–18).

## KEY SCRIPTURES

(Christ) is the image of the invisible God, the firstborn of every creature: [16] For by him were all things created, that are in heaven, and that are in earth.

**Col 1:15-16**

....in (Christ) dwelleth all the fulness of the Godhead bodily. [10] And ye are complete in him.

**Col 2:9, 10**

Let the word of Christ dwell in you richly [b]in all wisdom; teaching and admonishing one another in psalms and hymns and spiritual songs, singing with grace in your hearts to the Lord.

**Col 3:16**

Let your speech *be* alway with grace, seasoned with salt, that ye may know how ye ought to answer every man.

**Col 4:6**

KEY QUOTES

That these two letters (Ephesians and Colossians) have a close affinity is evident to any observant reader. Both were carried by the same messenger (Col 4:7-8; Eph 6:21-22). Both are greatly occupied with Christ and the church, which in Ephesians is viewed mostly in the universal rather than in the local sense. In Colossians the term *body* is preferred to *church*. Both letters magnify the headship of Christ over the body, but Colossians puts special emphasis on His supremacy in the cosmos, a truth not completely lacking from Ephesians (1:10, 21-22; 4:10). Both mention angelic powers. But, whereas Colossians was designed to meet the challenge of false teaching, Ephesians was written for spiritual edification. Many words, phrases, and even sentences are the same in both, suggesting that the two documents were written with only a brief interval between them.[38]

**Everett Harrison**

The epistle's main impact on subsequent theology has been through the exposition of the role of Christ in 1:15-20: from this developed the idea of the "cosmic Christ," emphasizing the key role played by Christ in both creation and redemption. Also influential has been the idea found in 2:11-15 of Christ's defeat of the cosmic powers at his death: from this developed the understanding of atonement known as "Christus Victor.[39]

**Morna Hooker**

---

[38]*Colossians: Christ All-sufficient* (Moody Press) p. 11..
[39]*Eerdmans Commentary on the Bible,* (Eerdmans) p. 1405.

## KEY QUESTIONS

1. What are the key similarities between Ephesians and Colossians?

2. Why did Paul use the word "fullness" so much in these letters?

3. Identify a verse in Colossians and a verse in Ephesians that is nearly identical.

4. How did the gospel reach Colossae?

# Chapter One

**Key Points**

- Salvation is manifested in faith, hope and love.

- The Church has been brought into greater blessings than those Israel enjoyed.

- The Lord Jesus is both God and Man; as such He is worthy of our devotion and praise.

- God's purpose to unite Jew and Gentile in the Church was not revealed prior to the teaching of the apostles.

## The Proofs of Salvation (vv1-8)

After a short greeting, the apostle opens his letter by seeking to encourage the Colossians. Though he had never met them he had heard about them from Epaphras (1:7). What he had heard was good. They had been saved and immediately begun to demonstrate the reality of their "faith" by their "love" for fellow Christians. Their faith and love was linked to "hope". Hope is the confident anticipation that one day they would be with the Lord in heaven. Paul places the work in Colossae in a larger context and rejoices in the progress of the gospel all over the world (cf. v23). The "world" he refers to is the world he knew. The world outside the Roman Empire and the countries around the Mediterranean were unknown or unpopulated.

## The Progress of Salvation (vv9-11)

One of the features of the Prison Epistles is that they open with prayer and the giving of thanks (Eph. 1:3; Phil. 1:3). Prayers are usually spoken.

This prayer is in writing. While we do not usually read prayers, Paul often put his prayers into writing. While the Lord Jesus warned his disciples not to make a public show of their prayers (Mt. 6:5), there is nothing wrong in telling people that we pray for them! Although our payers are usually about specific people and their needs this is a very general prayer. He prays that they might know God's will, that their lives would be pleasing to God and that they would be enabled by God's power to be patient in suffering and joyful in spirit. Listening to the prayer and worship of godly men is instructive. This prayer emphasises the need to know God's will and not to be marked by spiritual weakness.

## The Privileges of Salvation (vv12-14)
Like Ephesians, Colossians contains tremendous teaching about the blessings of salvation. Paul borrows from the O.T. and shows that the physical blessings that the nation of Israel enjoyed are paralleled by the spiritual blessings given to the Church. Israel was given an earthly inheritance in the form of a land in which the twelve tribes could live. The Church has been given a spiritual inheritance. Israel was a kingdom ruled over by David's dynasty. The Church is part of a kingdom ruled by Christ. Israel was redeemed from Egypt by the blood of the Passover lamb. The Church has been redeemed from the bondage of sin by the death of Christ.

## The Provider of Salvation (vv15-20)
The apostle then focusses on the Lord Jesus. It may be that he felt the Colossians needed to understand that the Lord Jesus was not a lesser being than God. He may have thought that they needed to understand what His relationship was to the mighty angels they had heard about. He sets before them the greatness of the One who shed His blood on the cross (vv14, 20) so that they might truly honour Him (v18). First, the Lord Jesus "is the image of the invisible God". We cannot see God the Father. But through incarnation the Son of God took on flesh and became the Son of Man. In His person He expressed all that God the Father was. He was the "image" or manifestation of God. Second, He was the "firstborn of every creature". As verse 16 shows, that this does not mean He was the first creature to be created. "Firstborn" is sometimes used in scripture in its secondary sense of someone who is first in rank and dignity (see e.g. Ps 89:27). He is firstborn in rank because He created all things. Paul is anxious to

draw attention to the fact that this means He created the angels.  No doubt he is anticipating an issue referred to later in the letter where he stresses His superiority to the "principalities and powers" (2:10, 15) so that the Colossians are not led into superstitious veneration of angels.  Third, he teaches His eternal existence (v17). While it is true He is "before" all things in rank, the succeeding phrase suggests that Paul is thinking of the fact that the Son of God first created and then sustained all things.  Fourth, as noted, He maintains all things. Without Him the universe would implode. Fifth, He is also supreme in the spiritual sphere. Paul's first four points relate to His priority in relation to the material creation. Now he sets out His in relation to the new creation. Here He is the head of the church.  Sixth, He is the first to rise from the dead and ascend in glory to heaven. Seventh, He is the One through whom God will subjugate everything to Himself. This anticipates a future reconciliation when all enemies have been removed and God rules without hindrance in the new creation.  This is brought about through the Lord's conquest at the end of the Millennium and His judicial disposal of all who have rebelled at the great white throne.

## The Peace of Salvation (vv21-22)
In contrast to the future reconciliation of all things, Christians are reconciled in the present. Usually when the New Testament speaks of the sacrifice it refers to blood. Here by contrast the body of the Lord is emphasised.  The eternal Son of God was a spirit and was not liable to death. After incarnation He became the Son of Man who was the subject of prophecy and took a body that could die. The effect of His body being offered in sacrifice was to enable the sanctification of the believer.  The emphasis here is not so much on practical sanctification but the ultimate sanctification of the believer when the Church is presented to Christ (v22).

## The Proclamation of Salvation (vv23-25)
Paul then speaks of the sufferings he has suffered because of his proclamation of the gospel (v23, 24).  Since he was in prison when he wrote this letter, he may have had this form of suffering in mind.  He describes them as Christ's sufferings not his sufferings. This does not mean that he had any part in the substitutionary sufferings of Christ on the cross since these were completed when the Lord cried "finished".  Instead he speaks of the sufferings that God has decreed His people

should pass through.  These are the sufferings of Christ's spiritual body, the church.  It must suffer before it is glorified.  Paul's sufferings are a consequence of being identified with a rejected Christ.  He describes himself as a minister or servant, first of the gospel (v23) and then of the church (v25).  His service consisted in proclaiming the gospel and serving the Lord's people. As a servant he humbly accepts the hardships his ministry brings.

## The Pre-eminence of Salvation (vv26-29)

There are many differences between Israel under Law and the Church under grace. One of the major differences of emphasis is that God's blessing under Law was largely though not exclusively focussed on Israel.  By contrast under grace God's blessing was for all people everywhere. Paul staggered at this change. All his years of training and study prior to salvation had taught him that Israel enjoyed privileged status.  There are many issues that are touched on in the O.T. and developed in the New Testament But the union of Jew and Gentile is not one of them. Paul describes the idea that God may conceal something and then reveal it as a "mystery". Paul asserts that his role is to proclaim the "mystery among the gentiles" (v27), that is the inclusion of all peoples in God's blessing notwithstanding the absence of any word from God to that effect in the O.T. The gospel message was a wonder to Paul because it entitled him to preach to "every man" (v28).  He was energised by the thought that through his efforts he could "present" those who once had been outsiders to Christ as a form of tribute.  The message of salvation eclipses any other message that might be preached.

KEY SCRIPTURES

....we heard of your faith in Christ Jesus, and of the love *which ye have* to all the saints, ⁵ For the hope which is laid up for you in heaven,

**Col 1:4-5**

...the Father, which hath made us meet to be partakers of the inheritance of the saints in light: ¹³ Who hath delivered us from the power of darkness, and hath translated *us* into the kingdom of his dear Son: ¹⁴ In whom we have redemption through his blood, *even* the forgiveness of sins.

**Col 1:12-14**

...he is before all things, and by him all things consist. ¹⁸ And he is the head of the body, the church: who is the beginning, the firstborn from the dead; that in all *things* he might have the preeminence.

**Col 1:17-18**

...the mystery that has been kept hidden from ages and generations, but has now been revealed to his saints. ¹:²⁷ God wanted to make known to them the glorious riches of this mystery among the Gentiles, which is Christ in you, the hope of glory.

**Col 1:26-27 NET.**

## KEY QUOTES

Creation is attributed to the Son. "All things were made through Him" (John 1.3, RV.). "By Him were all things created that are in heaven and that are in earth, visible and invisible, whether they be thrones, or dominions, or principalities, or powers: all things were created by Him and for Him, and by Him all things consist," or hold together (Col. 1.16,17). Not Himself a created being, as some infer, but before and above all created beings and things, their Creator and upholder— "upholding all things by the Word of His power" (Heb. 1.2), and by "the same word" the heavens and the earth are "kept in store, reserved unto fire" (2 Pet. 3.5,7). His mighty Word, which gave creation being, causes it to hold together, else, in spite of what sceptics call "the law of nature," it would collapse and fall to pieces. Could a mere creature, a man, do all this? Can the Creator and Upholder of all things be less than a Divine person, God the Son?[40]

**John Ritchie**

The life and ministry of the Lord Jesus was a constant manifestation of the power of the Creator, as demonstrated for example by His miracles (e.g. Mk. 4:41). There is nothing strange or incredible in this, for He Himself is the agent of all creation. Jesus is none other than the Creator entering His creation, so that He has only to speak and it is done (e.g. Mk. 3:5); also His word of command has creative power to produce obedience even from the dead (e.g. Mk. 5:41).[41]

**Dick Lucas**

---

[40]Rep. Assembly Testimony Jan/Feb. 1987.
[41]*The Bible Speaks Today - The Message of Colossians & Philemon: Fullness and freedom.* (IVP) p. 50.

## KEY QUESTIONS

1. Are Christians part of a kingdom as well as belonging to the Church? Whose kingdom do we belong to?

2. In what sense is Christ the "firstborn"?

3. In what sense is Christ the "image of the invisible God"?

4. What does the reconciliation of the Christian involve?

# Chapter Two

**Key Points**

- True fulfilment and enlightenment is to be found in Christ.

- The Lord Jesus was fully man and fully God.

- Baptism symbolises that we have died to our old life and have been raised to new life in Christ.

- We should remain loyal to Christ and avoid mixing Christianity with other religions that deny Him.

**The Crisis for the Church** – Paul evidently foresaw problems for the Colossian church. He was concerned that someone might "beguile" (v4) and "spoil" them (v8). This concern led to great "conflict" (*agona* – v1) within him. This probably refers to deep spiritual concern rather than physical sufferings. He must have heard that there were people seeking to influence the Colossians. Thankfully they had not succumbed to the false teaching (v5) but Paul evidently thought there was a risk.

If ch 1 underlines the supremacy of Christ, ch 2 gives us an explanation of why Paul felt it necessary to expound the supremacy of the Lord Jesus. First, there were those who wanted to re-impose the O.T. Law on the Christians at Colossae. Paul had no objection to the moral and spiritual values of the O.T. and indeed restates some of them in this chapter e.g. "thou shalt not bear false witness" (Ex. 20:16; Col 3:9). He did however repudiate the rites and ceremonies of

THE PRISON EPISTLES   101

the O.T.  His objection is laid bare in v 16. Any one who is familiar with the Acts of the Apostles or Galatians will know how hard Paul fought against those who sought to impose the Law on new Gentile converts.  As he says in v 17, why go back to the shadows of the Law when in the Lord Jesus we have the "body" i.e. the substance. Why gaze at the shadow when you can gaze at the One who cast the shadow? .

But there were other influences at work. It seems that the Colossians were being encouraged to worship angels (v18). While other parts of the New Testament stress Christ's supremacy over angels (e.g. Heb. 1) this is the only occasion where we read of anyone actually teaching they were worthy of worship.  The point of 1:16 is now obvious.  Ch 2:10 stresses the Lord Jesus is the "head of all principality and power".

Another influence which was pressing on the Colossians is what is usually called asceticism.  Asceticism is found in many religions including Hinduism and Buddhism.  Christendom embraced it wholeheartedly for many centuries. Asceticism is basically a lifestyle characterised by abstinence from worldly pleasure.  Up to a point this is good. The Lord Jesus lived a simple lifestyle as did John Baptist. But asceticism can be carried to extremes. In v23 we learn that the Colossians were being taught that they should neglect their bodies. Presumably this refers to prolonged fasting, flagellation and other forms of behaviour that damage the body. There is a balance between self-indulgence and self-harm. The body is the "temple of the Holy Spirit" (1 Cor. 6:19) and is not to be abused. It may be that this type of teaching had its root in the idea that the body is inherently evil (vv. 22-23) which was part of a teaching called Gnosticism. This may be the "philosophy" of v8. Gnosticism taught that all matter is evil and that to bridge the gap between the material world populated by humans and God there were a host of intermediate beings the lowest of which created a world of evil matter.  Probably the angels mentioned in Colossians are these intermediate beings.

As he states in the opening section of the chapter, Christians function properly when their hearts (v2) and minds (v2b) are absorbed with Christ.  A common appreciation of Christ leads to stability (v6) and fulfilment (v10).

**The Challenge to the Church –** one of the hallmarks of Colossians is that Paul uses words and concepts associated with these false teachings. Paul's aim in using the terminology of these rival belief systems was probably to accentuate the differences between Christianity and these rival systems. For example, circumcision was a prominent sign of adherence to the Law. Under the Law children were circumcised when eight days old (Gen. 17:12). Paul does not say circumcision is wrong as such, though he would probably have categorised it along with the matters mentioned in v16. Instead he speaks about the "circumcision made without hands" (v11) and the "circumcision of Christ" (v11b) i.e. the circumcision performed by Christ. Paul teaches that salvation involved the "circumcision" or cutting off of the root cause of sin and not just a portion of human flesh. This new circumcision was accomplished by Christ when He died on the cross. He is not of course teaching that after salvation we cease to have the capacity to sin but he is teaching that through salvation we are no longer to be judged or governed by the nature inherited from Adam.

Another example of Paul utilising his opponents' ideas is his use of the words "fullness" (1:9, 19; 2:9) and "knowledge" (1:9, 10; 2:2, 3). Gnosticism was a system of religious thought that involved gradual growth in enlightenment by being initiated into secret knowledge. Its adherents in acquiring secret knowledge achieved spiritual enlightenment. Now of course Christianity also encourages growing knowledge. But it teaches that the only knowledge that matters is knowledge of Christ. Hence even the greatest philosophers cannot compare to Christ (v8). Paul's aim is to make the Colossians appreciate that any system of religion or philosophy of life that does not have Christ at its heart is worthless. He is like a treasure trove (v2, 3). The Greeks believed that knowledge was valuable. Greek culture had given the world some of its greatest philosophers. But their nuggets of wisdom were nothing in comparison to the wealth to be found in Christ. The Greek gods they worshipped had a human form but were marked by weakness and vice. Christ took up humanity but in doing so displayed the full attributes of deity (v9). If they were tempted to worship angels Paul says they would do well to remember that Christ was not only the creator of all creatures (including angels) but He was their "head" or superior (v10). As concerning the Judaising teachers, the rituals of the O.T. had been superseded by Christ.

**The Centre of the Church –** we have noticed that ch 1:15-18 sets out the reasons for the pre-eminence of the Lord Jesus. That famous section begins with the statement that He is "the image of the invisible God" and ends with "it pleased the Father that in Him should all fullness dwell". Ch 2:9 picks up this theme and states that "the fullness of the godhead" or "the fullness of deity" (E.S.V.) dwells in Him. The point here is that all the attributes of deity dwell in the man Christ Jesus. The point is that in taking up a human body and becoming man He did not lose any of the attributes of deity and these dwell in Him. If that is the case any system of religion that displaced Him should be shunned. Judaism rejected His deity and resurrection from the dead. If so, those that sought to force the Colossians to accept a religion of circumcision, feasts and sabbaths should be rejected. Likewise if there were philosophers that had no place for Christ in their view of the world they too should be rejected. If teachers asked them to worship angels the Colossians should worship the creator of the angels instead. In ch 1:18 He is described as the "head of the Church". In ch 2:10 He is the "head of all principality and power" i.e. the mighty angels. In 2:19 He is again presented as the Head of the Church but here He does not just control the body (the Church), He supplies power and energy to it. For this reason Christians are told to "hold" or remain connected to the Head who keeps the whole body united together.

The Colossians in their baptism allied themselves to the Lord Jesus (2:12). The One who had "circumcised" them (see above) was the One with whom they had become identified in His death, burial and resurrection. On salvation we too died to the world and emerged in a new life. Baptism (which occurs after salvation) was a symbolic declaration of these facts.

His death on the cross is described as similar to a series of debts being cancelled (2:14). The expression "handwriting of ordinances" was an expression in use at the time to mean a list of debts accumulated by a debtor. These debts were not monetary debts but spiritual debts involving breaches of God's law. Paul uses a striking metaphor. He writes not of Christ being crucified but the debts being crucified. The nailing of the debts to the cross symbolised their payment and consequent extinction.

Hence the point of the chapter is to force the Colossians to realise the centrality of Christ. Any one or anything that diminishes His status or displaces His role in the Church is to be rejected.

## KEY SCRIPTURES

....Christ; In whom are hid all the treasures of wisdom and knowledge.

**Col 2:2-3**

...in him dwelleth all the fulness of the Godhead bodily. ¹⁰ And ye are complete in him, which is the head of all principality and power:

**Col 2:9-10**

¹⁶ Let no man therefore judge you in meat, or in drink, or in respect of an holyday, or of the new moon, or of the sabbath *days*: ¹⁷ Which are a shadow of things to come; but the body *is* of Christ.

**Col 2:16-17**

KEY QUOTES

... in Jesus are hidden all the treasures of *wisdom* and *knowledge*. Wisdom is *sophia*, and knowledge is *gnōsis*. These two words do not simply repeat each other; there is a difference between them. *Gnōsis* is the power, almost intuitive and instinctive, to grasp the truth when we see it and hear it. But *sophia* is the power to confirm and to commend the truth with wise and intelligent argument, once it has been intuitively grasped. *Gnōsis* is that by which people grasp the truth; *sophia* is that by which people are enabled to give a reason for the hope that is in them.

All this wisdom, says Paul, is *hidden* in Christ. The word he uses for *hidden* is *apokruphos*. His very use of that word is a blow aimed at the Gnostics. *Apokruphos* means *hidden from the common gaze*, and therefore *secret*. ... the Gnostics believed that a great mass of elaborate knowledge was necessary for salvation. That knowledge they set down in their books, which they called *apokruphos* because they were barred to ordinary people. By using this one word, Paul is saying: 'You Gnostics have your wisdom hidden from ordinary people; we too have our knowledge, but it is not hidden in unintelligible books; it is hidden in Christ and therefore open to all men and women everywhere.'[42]

**William Barclay**

---

[42] *The Letters to Philippians, Colossians, and Thessalonians* 3rd ed. (Westminster John Knox Press.) p. 151.

## KEY QUOTES

In Christ dwells all the fulness (completeness) of the absolute Godhead, essentially and perfectly: The very Personality of God. As W. Kelly points out, "the fulness of the Godhead never dwelt in the Father *bodily*, or in the Holy Ghost, but only in Christ." God is known because of incarnation: Hence, "in Him dwelleth all the fulness of the Godhead *bodily*." There is nothing speculative here. The Lord Jesus is "God ... manifest in the flesh" 1 Tim.3.16. It is He of Whom John wrote: "That which was from the beginning, which we have heard, which we have seen with our eyes, which we have looked upon, and our hands have handled, of the Word of life" 1 Jn.1.1.[43]

**John Riddle**

---

[43]*The Glory of the Son* ch 2 "The Deity of His Person" (Assembly Testimony Publication) p. 25.

## KEY QUESTIONS

1. What false teaching were the Colossians exposed to?

2. If Christians no longer need to be physically circumcised, in what sense are Christians circumcised in Colossians?

3. In Colossians ch 3 what teaching does Paul give about the symbolism of baptism?

4. What does the expression "handwriting of ordinances" mean and in what way was it nailed to the cross?

# Chapter Three

**Key Points**

- A Christian should be focussed on heaven and its values.

- A Christian should not be marked by sexual immorality or bad language.

- Christians express their faith in hymns which both praise God and express the great truths of Christianity.

- The Christian household is marked by submission and love.

In chapter three, Paul moves away from the religious dangers of chapter two and looks at the moral dangers faced by the Colossians.

## A Heavenly Mind

Paul writes of things above (3:1, 2) and contrasts them with the things that are "on earth" (3:5). Although he does not identify the heavenly "things" he probably has in mind the virtues described in vv12-17. These are the characteristics of heaven.

## A Hidden Life

As in chapter two (2:12, 13, 20) Paul encourages the Colossians to think of themselves as identified with the Lord Jesus in His death and resurrection (3:1, 3).[44] He tells them to focus on the day that they will be revealed from heaven with Him (3:4). What does Paul mean by this? The idea seems to be that although our bodies are on earth in every other

---

[44]The other idea is that the Christian is "as good as" raised and glorified in God's mind and is treated as such.

respect, we should live as if we had left the world behind and been raised with the Lord Jesus to heaven. Though our bodies are earth bound, our hearts and spirits should be fastened to the Lord. We should think of ourselves as those who are with Him in spirit. On death our souls will join Him. In the resurrection our bodies will be raised to be where He is. At the Second Coming what has been hidden from the world's view will be revealed (3:3, 4). Christ is hidden and He will be revealed.  The Christian too is hidden in a different sense.  Sometimes in the Bible that which is "hidden" is that which cannot be understood (Lk 9:45). We are an enigma to the world and have values and ambitions that it cannot comprehend. Our lives are "hid".

## A Holy Walk

Chapter three is characterised by lists of vices and virtues.  The first list of vices is in 3:5 and the second is in 3:8.  The first list sets out things that must put to death ("mortify" v5 A.V.) and it consists primarily of immoral deeds. The second list sets out things that must be put off like dirty clothes (3:8) and consists of immoral words. In total there are eleven vices. The nature of the sin is clear in most cases but some require explanation –

- "fornication" - sexual immorality of all sorts including adultery and pre-marital sex. In other contexts the words fornication and adultery appear together. On the reasonable assumption that the two words refer to different things, there fornication means pre-marital sex and adultery unfaithfulness within the marriage bond.
- "uncleanness" – a wide term for immoral behaviour of whatever kind. Although Paul had never heard of the internet he would undoubtedly have regarded watching online pornography as "uncleanness".
- "inordinate affection" – these two English words translate one word Greek word which means "passion".  The context here indicates that Paul means sinful passion.
- "evil concupiscence" – this also is one word in the Greek text. It also means passion or lust. While the word can refer to a good desire e.g. Lk. 22:15 "with <u>desire</u> I have desired to eat this Passover with you", here it means evil desire.

By contrast the heavenly virtues are listed in one large group (v12). If evil is to be cast off like dirty clothes virtue is to be put on like clean clothes (3:10, 12). These virtues include kindness, humility, meekness, patience, toleration and forgiveness. He likens love to a belt that holds the other garments in place (3:14).

## A Healed Humanity

Paul also says that Christians have "put off" the "old man" (3:9). This is an unusual metaphor. Had he said "mortify" that would be easier to follow since a "man" can be killed. Paul is probably using the word "put off" in a similar way to "mortify" in v5 since "put off" can mean "to strip off violently". It is used in 2:15 of what the Lord Jesus did when He "spoiled" principalities and powers in the sense that He stripped them of power.

Putting off the "old man" is part of a rich and varied set of descriptions in scripture of what happens at salvation. [45] The "new man" is a new status which we receive because of our new relationship with Christ. But it has a practical aspect as well since on salvation we put off the "deeds" (v9) of the old man. The "new man" is "put on" (3:10) at the same time. Paul teaches that this was a once for all act (cf. Eph. 4:22-24; Rom. 6:6). The "old man" is to be distinguished from, although closely connected to, the flesh which continues to reside within Christians as a kind of legacy of the "old man".

Being made a new man brings entry into a new society where the ethnic, religious and social distinctions that divide humanity are erased (3:11). The legacy of the first Adam is supplanted by the last Adam (1 Cor 15:45). In the beginning man had been made in God's image (Gen. 1:27), but because of the Fall that image was disfigured. The Fall also brought a knowledge of sin (Gen. 3:5, 22). The new man thrives through knowing Christ (3:10). As his knowledge of God deepens so the image of God becomes clearer. The humanity that was ruined in the Fall is healed.

The new community ought to be marked by the virtues listed in v 12. They are "elect" (*eklectoi*) which means chosen. They are "holy", which means set apart. Holiness is an aspect of salvation which constitutes believers "saints" or holy

---

[45]On salvation God "stripped off" the "old man" (what we were in Adam) and "put on" the "new man" (what we are in Christ). But what we are by standing we should also be by state. Salvation made us "new creatures" (2 Cor 5:17; Gal 6:15) and gave us new birth (Jn 3:3, 7; 1 Pet 1:23; 2:2).

ones as well as a state of practical holiness. These chosen saints are "beloved" of God.

## A Harmonious Song

In contrast to the war and tumult wrought by sin, believers have peace (v15). They are also marked by song (v16).  These are not the empty songs of the world but give expression to the truth of the word of Christ.  The Church did not abandon Israel's ancient hymnbook the Psalms but added to them "hymns and spiritual songs". This indicates that new compositions were circulated designed to give expression to truths absent from the Psalms. In the New Testament the writers quote from snatches of the new songs composed to express the new truth of the Church era (e.g. 2 Tim. 2:11-13).  It is evident that melody is not the key issue, though a good tune always helps!  These songs are vehicles designed to express vital truth and to praise the Lord. While it is good to enjoy hymns we must be careful they do not become a form of entertainment – that is far removed from their original purpose (3:16-17).

## A Happy Home

The letter ends with a description of how the Christian should live at home whether as a husband, wife, child, master or slave. Ephesians has a similar section (5:22-6:9). The six categories of people are arranged in pairs.  In each case there is a relationship of subordination. The wife submits to the husband, the child to the parent and the slave to the master. The reciprocal duties are respectively of love, care and respect.  Although the Scriptures teach the equality of man with woman (Gal 3:28; 1 Cor. 11:11-12; cf. 3:11) submission is enjoined as the proper attitude of the wife to her husband, in the same way that the Son is submissive to the Father's will without being His inferior. Because the relationship is based on love the submission of the wife is not marked by ideas of inferiority on the part of the wife or dominance on the part of the husband.  The child likewise submits.  As a husband must not take advantage of his position, so a parent must be sensitive to the child and not do anything that would turn the child against the parent (3:21).  As he deals with the relationship of slaves and masters Paul enlarges his perspective to include all believers.  Whatever a believer does he ought to do as if it was service for God. His life is not compartmented. He ought to be anxious to show in his life the difference salvation has made. He recognises that the true assessor of his life is God Himself (3:24, 25). The section concludes in 4:1 with a revolutionary principle. Christian masters should not be content to follow the standards of the day in deciding what to pay or how to treat their slaves.  If that is so with slaves the same can be said of employees or people whom Christians engage to do work for them. They should not give as little as they can but give what is "just and equal". "Just" means fair "Equal" means giving equal pay for equal work.

 ## KEY SCRIPTURES

If ye then be risen with Christ, seek those things which are above, where Christ sitteth on the right hand of God.

**Col 3:1**

...ye have put off the old man with his deeds; And have put on the new *man*, which is renewed in knowledge after the image of him that created him:

**Col 3:9-10**

Let the word of Christ dwell in you richly in all wisdom; teaching and admonishing one another in psalms and hymns and spiritual songs, singing with grace in your hearts to the Lord.

**Col 3:16**

Children, obey *your* parents in all things: for this is well pleasing unto the Lord. Fathers, provoke not your children *to anger*, lest they be discouraged.

**Col 3:20–21**

## KEY QUOTES

Ascension follows resurrection: hence, if we are the members of Christ we must ascend into heaven, because He, on being raised up from the dead, was *received up into heaven*, (Mark 16:19,) that He might draw us up with Him. Now, we *seek those things which are above*, when in our minds we are truly sojourners in this world, and are not bound to it. The word rendered *think upon* expresses rather assiduity and intensity of aim: "Let your whole meditation be as to this: to this apply your intellect — to this your mind." But if we ought to think of nothing but of what is heavenly, because Christ is in heaven, how much less becoming were it to seek Christ upon the earth. Let us therefore bear in mind that *that* is a true and holy *thinking* as to Christ, which forthwith bears us up into heaven, that we may there adore Him, and that our minds may dwell with Him.

**John Calvin**[46]

Children have rights, but they also have responsibilities; and their foremost responsibility is to obey. They are to obey "in all things" and not simply in those things that please them. Will their parents ever ask them to do something that is wrong? Not if the parents are submitted to the Lord and to one another, and not if they love each other and their children.

The child who does not learn to obey his parents is not likely to grow up obeying *any* authority. He will defy his teachers, the police, his employers, and anyone else who tries to exercise authority over him. The breakdown in authority in our society reflects the breakdown of authority in the home.

**Warren Wiersbe**[47]

[46]Calvin's Commentaries.
[47]*The Bible Exposition Commentary* (Victor Books) Vol. 2 p. 143.

## KEY QUESTIONS

1. What influence does the fact that Christians are bound for heaven have on their lives on earth?

2. Who or what is the "old man"?

3. Give some practical examples of the way in which a wife might submit to her husband? Give some practical examples of the way in which a husband could show love for his wife?

4. Does Paul teach that there should be "equal pay for equal work"?

# Chapter Four

## Key Points

- We should pray that God would use us to spread the gospel.

- Our speech should be edifying and clean.

- If an assembly hears that one of the Lord's servants is in distress, it should seek to help if it can.

- It is good to have an interest in the wellbeing of other Christians.

**Practical Issues**

Paul ends with an encouragement to pray. He began the letter by praying and giving thanks for the Colossians (1:3, 9 and 12) and now he exhorts the Colossians to do the same for him (4:2). The issues he is interested in are still issues we pray for today. He asks them to pray that he will be able to communicate the gospel ("the mystery of Christ"). While we may not be in prison we too ought to have a desire to pass the gospel on. For Paul his audience was probably the Roman soldiers who guarded him and prisoners he met while being processed by the Roman legal system. He also encourages them to pray about their everyday life. He knows that Christians are prone to wasting time. Paul realised that time was a valuable commodity which needed to be "redeemed" (4:5). In other words it needed to be bought back from the service of the world or personal interests and put into God's service. One valuable use of time is to live a godly life (4:5) and to speak in a way that is God honouring (4:6).  The Christian should not swear or tell doubtful stories. They should always be truthful and where possible express their faith in Christ.  This is what makes speech "salty". Salt is used to preserve food. Salt also gives flavour to food. So the Christian's speech should never lead to others being corrupted in any way and should be truthful and honest.  This gives Christian conversation a distinctive and palatable flavour.

**Private Matters**
One of the major differences between Colossians and Ephesians is that it ends with some personal references and a long list of greetings to a variety of people. Ephesians lacks that personal touch.  Before launching into the greeting list, Paul refers to Tychicus who had been sent from Colossae to Rome to meet with him either in his "hired house" (Acts 28:30) or if at a later stage of his time in Rome, in his cell in the Royal Palace (Phil. 1:13; 4:22).  He may have come with a gift or to pass on the greetings and encouragement of the Colossians.  He is now on his way back to Colossae probably as the bearer of the letter to the church at Colossae. He is commended highly by Paul as a "beloved brother" which speaks of Paul's affection for him, a "faithful minister" which speaks of his fidelity to God and to the church at Colossae and lastly as a "fellowservant" which speaks of Paul's fellowship with him in the work of God. Paul also refers to Onesimus. More is said of him in the letter to Philemon which was also sent back with Tychicus. We will deal with them in the last chapter of these Notes.  During Paul's various imprisonments he received a variety of support and practical encouragement from Christians.  Today Christians are still being imprisoned or martyred for their faith and we should have a desire to support them if we can.

**Personal Greetings**
In total ten individuals are mentioned at the close of the letter.  Paul often greets people by name or conveys their greetings to his audience. Romans ch 16 is a prime example of this. Here in Colossians he has a comment about nearly everyone.  This demonstrates his personal interest in people and his wide circle of friends and acquaintances.

The fact that Aristarchus is a fellow prisoner indicates that Paul was not the only Christian in Rome on criminal charges. Whether Aristarchus had also appealed to Rome in order to determine whether the governors of the Roman province of Judea had jurisdiction to try someone who was a Roman citizen is not stated. He may have faced different charges and a different court. "Marcus" is referred to elsewhere as Mark. This reference sheds light on the issue which arose in Acts 15:37-39 between Paul and Barnabas. It seems that even in the work of the Lord "blood is thicker than water". Barnabas may well have been influenced by his family relationship with Mark in wanting to take him on the missionary journey. In any event, rather tragically Paul and Barnabas fell out and never worked together again. This should be a warning that family ties can lead good men to make bad judgements about spiritual matters.

The reference to Jesus is interesting because it shows that the Lord's name was not unique to the Lord. It is the Greek form of the Hebrew name "Joshua". Some societies today e.g. in Brazil and Spain, continue to use the name "Jesus" as a name for children. He may have been re-named Justus because the Christians were not comfortable with someone being known by the same name as their Lord. Paul indicates that all these men are of the "circumcision" i.e. Jews (v11) and that they were the only Jews who had been of assistance to him during his confinement. We may therefore deduce that the other people he names are Gentiles and that Gentile Christians had become the main source of support for the apostle.

These include Epaphras. The phrase "who is one of you" indicates he was from Colossae. He sends his greetings to the Colossians. It is therefore evident that he was not travelling with Tychicus and had remained in Rome with Paul. Laodicea and Hierapolis were towns that neighboured Colossae. It seems therefore his sphere of labour was not only his home assembly but the locality as well.

The reference to Luke provides us with some background information on the man who wrote Luke's gospel and the Acts of the Apostles (cf. 2 Tim 4:11). Because of their length these two books make Luke the most prolific New Testament writer (if Hebrews was not written by Paul). Despite that we know little about him. Here we are told that he was a medical doctor. This would have made him an invaluable help to Paul given the physical pounding he took during his missionary work (Acts 14:19) and the health problems that beset him (2 Cor

12:7).  It is noticeable that although he calls Luke "beloved" he says nothing about Demas (v14). Paul may have had a premonition that Demas would not prove faithful (2 Tim 4:10).

Nymphas (some manuscripts suggest that this is a female name) like other believers in the early days of the Church used his house as the meeting place for the assembly (Philemon 2, cf. Rom. 16:5; 1 Cor 16:19). Most Christians leave their home to go to the church. Nymphas remained at home. No doubt the meetings were disruptive. Rooms would have to be cleared and furniture rearranged.  His neighbours would be in no doubt that he was associated with the Christians. Using his home in this way was quite a sacrifice to make.

Paul closes by seeking to secure a wide circulation for the letter (v16) and refers to another letter he wrote to the assembly at Laodicea – what it said or what became of it is unknown. Paul's remarks indicate that he did not just intend his letters to be read by their immediate recipients.  This is obvious in his letters to Timothy where many of his comments do not readily apply to the addressee of the letter but are plainly directed to Christians generally. The final comment is addressed to a man called Archippus. He does not state what "ministry" (v17) Archippus had received.  Whatever it was, Paul desired him to fulfil it.  This is true for us all. We have all a role to play in the work of God. The challenge is to fulfil it.

**KEY SCRIPTURES**

Continue in prayer, and watch in the same with thanksgiving;

**Col 4:2**

Let your speech *be* alway with grace, seasoned with salt, that ye may know how ye ought to answer every man.

**Col 4:6**

Luke, the beloved physician, and Demas, greet you.

**Col 4:17**

Say to Archippus, Take heed to the ministry which thou hast received in the Lord, that thou fulfil it.

**Col 4:17**

**KEY QUOTES**

"Let *your speech be always with grace*, v. 6. Let all your discourse be as becomes Christians, suitable to your profession-savoury, discreet, seasonable." Though it be not always <u>of</u> grace, it must be always <u>with</u> grace; and, though the matter of our discourse be that which is common, yet there must be an air of piety upon it and it must be in a Christian manner *seasoned with salt*. Grace is the salt which seasons our discourse, makes it savoury, and keeps it from corrupting.[48]

**Matthew Henry**

As Paul concludes his epistle to the Colossians ... A message is to be given to Archippus, ... This message was terse: "And say to Archippus, Take heed to the ministry which thou hast received in the Lord, that thou fulfil it" (Col 4.17), perhaps indicating that Paul did not expect him to be present as the letter was read to the saints. Archippus is described by Paul in the letter to Philemon as "our fellowsoldier" (v.2), and by this description it is clear that he had laboured faithfully in the past..... The admonition seems to indicate that this "fellowsoldier" of the apostle may have been slacking in his diligence. The reason for this is unknown, but the fact that Paul makes this request in such a public manner indicates that Archippus' carelessness was a serious matter...

---

[48] Matthew Henry's commentary on the whole Bible: complete and unabridged in one volume (Hendrickson) p. 2336.

## KEY QUOTES

In assemblies we meet some who have never performed to their potential, and others who seemed to do so in the past, but no longer show the interest that once was theirs. The reasons are many. Some have become tired of the pressure of working in an assembly where they are little appreciated; some may have let the world encroach on their lives and that has caused the fire of devotion to grow cold; some may be affected by the apparent lack of response from others in the work in which they are engaged; some have let bitterness hold them in its vice-like grip; perhaps disputes have blunted the old fervour, or it may be that problems with which they have been faced have sucked the spiritual enthusiasm from them. No matter the cause, the servant is now under-performing. The assembly suffers, the family of the servant suffers, those who may benefit from the work suffer, and the servant suffers personally.[49]

**John Grant**

---

[49]"Character Studies in the Assembly" Believer's Magazine June 2005.

## KEY QUESTIONS

1. How did Paul manage to preach the gospel if he was in prison?

2. How many people does Paul mention in ch 4? Can we say who were Jews and who were Gentiles?

3. What background information does scripture give us about Mark?

4. What sort of "ministry" might Archippus have had?

# Philemon

**Key Points**

- Salvation requires us to treat others especially fellow Christians with respect.

- God at times allows problems into our lives with a view to the blessing of others.

- Those that are saved should seek to rectify wrongs done in their unsaved days.

- We should be willing to make financial sacrifices to help fellow Christians in difficulty.

## The Place of the Letter

The letter of Paul to Philemon is one of the shortest books in the bible. Although it is located just after the letters to Timothy and Titus (probably because the compiler of the canon wanted to keep Paul's short letters together) it really sits alongside the prison epistles – Ephesians, Philippians and Colossians. Although the letter does not say it was written at the same time as Colossians this seems likely. Paul is a prisoner (v9), as he is in Colossians, and the people he mentions in the greetings section at the end of the letter to the Colossians are basically the same group as he mentions in the letter to Philemon. In particular he mentions Onesimus in Colossians (Col. 4:9) who he says is "one of you" i.e. one of the Colossians to whom he wrote. Onesimus likewise features prominently in Philemon so it is reasonable to conclude that the two letters are linked. In the letter to Philemon it emerges that Onesimus was a slave (v16) who had had run away (v15) from Philemon his master.

Paul evidently assumes that this has caused Philemon financial loss (v18) possibly through the loss of Onesimus's services and the consequent need to hire alternative labour or possibly because Onesimus had stolen from Philemon – we don't really know.

**The Point of the Letter**
The main point of the letter is to patch up the relationship between Onesimus and Philemon.  Paul has met Onesimus while a prisoner and communicated the gospel with the result that Onesimus has been converted (vv. 10, 16).  Paul thought that Onesimus should return to his Master (v12).  His reasons are not explained but it seems likely that Paul recognised that this was the law. He no doubt also thought that since Philemon was a Christian there was no reason why Onesimus should not go back and put things right.  But he was sent back not so much as Philemon's slave but as a new brother.  While the letter does not examine the institution of slavery it is evident that Paul expects Philemon to treat Onesimus in a favourable way.  Many have suggested that if Philemon took Paul's entreaties to heart he would have freed Onesimus.  While Paul does not say so, he probably hoped that Philemon would see that the idea of a Christian owning another Christian as an item of property was inconsistent with human dignity and with the relationship that ought to exist between Christians. However that may be, Paul's main aim was to ensure a good reception for Onesimus. He offers to pay any costs caused by Onesimus's departure (v19). Paul also stresses how useful Onesimus had been to him while he was imprisoned (vv 11, 13). What exactly Onesimus had done for Paul is unspecified.  How they had met is also unclear.  Onesimus might have picked up work in the prison or courts in Rome. He may have been arrested and shared a cell with Paul.  We should not assume that Paul remained in the hired house mentioned at the end of Acts (Acts 28:30). The indications in Philippians are that he was in close confinement during the trial process (Phil 1:13, 4:22) so he may have met Onesimus then.  Whether the Roman authorities knew Onesimus was a runaway slave is doubtful.  The indications in this letter are that until Paul wrote to him Philemon was unaware of the whereabouts of Onesimus.  If so he would hardly have placed the Roman authorities on the "look out".

In interceding for Onesimus Paul refrains from issuing Philemon with any instructions. Paul knew that what Philemon did with Onesimus was for Philemon. Under law he was Philemon's property. Although he was an apostle and although Philemon had been converted through Paul's ministry (v19) he refrains from telling Philemon what to do. In Colossians we learned that Paul had never visited Colossae so although Philemon was resident there he must have encountered the apostle while away from home.

**The Puzzles in the Letter**
There are intriguing features in the letter. Paul asks Philemon to prepare him lodgings (v22). This assumes that he will be released and make his way to Colossae. It also assumes imminent release – if he was not likely to be in Colossae for some time, why make ready? What basis did Paul have for thinking he would be released? It may be that the trial process was nearing its conclusion and that the indications were that he would be released, possibly on conditions (see Phil 1:19, 25) although the possibility of capital punishment could not be ruled out (Phil 1:20-24). If Paul was about to be released he seems to have decided to travel to Asia Minor where Colossae was situated. This is a long journey so the lodgings may have been prepared for some time before he finally arrived. On the other hand we do not know how quickly the letter to Philemon took to reach its destination. It was probably carried by Tychicus and Onesimus the bearers of the letter to the Colossians (Col. 4:7-9).

**The Preservation of the Letter**
Why is this little letter in the canon of Scripture? It was probably kept initially because it achieved its purpose. Philemon probably did receive Onesimus as a brother. Philemon no doubt marvelled that God had ordered things so that his slave would meet Paul and be saved through him, even though Onesimus was hundreds of miles away from Colossae. For these reasons the letter may have been kept by Philemon. It may even have been kept by the "church in his house" (v2). Of course the supervising hand of the Spirit also preserved the letter. As Colossians 4:16 makes clear not everything Paul wrote was preserved.

**The Purposes of the Letter**
If Paul's immediate goal was to protect Onesimus and to encourage Philemon to

receive him again what was the Holy Spirit's purpose in inspiring and preserving the letter for the benefit of the Church?  There are a few possibilities.  First, It shines a light on how we should conduct ourselves when dealing with fellow Christians.  While Paul evidently thought Philemon should forgive Onesimus's past indiscretions he did not dictate to Philemon that he should do so.  He therefore seeks to persuade Philemon to forget the past and rejoice in the salvation of his runaway slave.  Paul even relies on his advanced years as a means of persuasion (v9).  His aim may not be to excite Philemon's pity but to rely on his respect for his age and experience.  In the days in which Paul wrote age was highly respected.  So too today we should respect the advice of older saints.  We should rejoice in God's work in salvation and be ready to forget the past.

The letter also shows how willing Paul was to put himself "on the line" for Christians. He offers to meet any costs caused by Philemon's wrongdoing (v18) even though he could not know exactly what the liability was.  He identifies closely with Onesimus (v12) even though in social terms he was nothing but a runaway slave.  Although Paul was an apostle with huge personal authority and a privileged upbringing, he was a friend of slaves. We too should have the same spirit.

The letter also shows how God can bring good out of calamities and wrongdoing. Onesimus should not have run away. Paul does not try to persuade Onesimus to remain in Rome with him. He knows that if someone breaks the law and does wrong it must be put right. Although Philemon would have been put out by Onesimus's departure, verse 15 makes it clear that God was at work. Although he seemed to have run away from Philemon, the departure was with a view to an eternal reunion.

Some have suggested that the letter to Philemon shows Paul's opposition to slavery.  This reads too much into the text.  While he argues that Onesimus should be viewed as a brother and not a chattel, he leaves it to Philemon to discern whether it is seemly for a Christian to own a slave.  While slavery is to be deplored Paul did not tackle the institution of slavery. Had he done so he would have been seen as challenging the State. It is estimated that at the time of writing approximately one third of all persons under Roman rule were slaves.

The Empire depended economically on slaves. To challenged slavery would have been to move the focus of the gospel away from spiritual enslavement to economic enslavement. Sadly many centuries rolled by before slavery collapsed.

 ## KEY SCRIPTURES

I am appealing to you concerning my child, whose spiritual father I have become during my imprisonment, that is, Onesimus, who was formerly useless to you, but is now useful to you and me. I have sent him (who is my very heart) back to you.

**Philemon vv 10-12 (NET)**

without thy mind would I do nothing.

**Philemon v 14**

perhaps he therefore departed for a season, that thou shouldest receive him for ever; [16] not now as a servant, but above a servant, a brother beloved

**Philemon vv 15, 16**

**KEY QUOTES**

..... the meaning of Onesimus is "profitable", but alas, like many others with a good name, he had failed to fulfil the hopes of those who named him. Indeed he had proved to be the direct opposite. However, now that he was converted, he could be relied upon to be a blessing wherever he might be. He was a monument to the power of the gospel, for it alone can change "wasters" into useful men and women...... [W]hen Paul instructs Philemon to receive his slave for "love's sake", he might well be thinking of the fact that "Philemon" means "loving one", and so he is asking him to live up to his good name. .... Other occasions in Scripture where there is a play upon the meaning of names will readily come to mind, such as in the case of Jacob, whose name means "supplanter", being described by his brother as acting true to his name in that he has supplanted him twice (Gen 27:36). In contrast to this is the case of Jabez, whose name means "sorrow", when he prayed that he might be kept from the evil that it be not to his sorrow (1 Chron 4:10 RV). Perhaps the most outstanding example of the importance of names and their meanings concerns the Seven Churches in Asia (Rev 2-3). Most are agreed that there is a link between the meaning of their respective names and the messages addressed to each.[50]

**Albert McShane**

[50]*What the Bible teaches - Galatians, Ephesians, Philippians, Colossians, Philemon* (John Ritchie Ltd.) p. 396.

## KEY QUOTES

I⊤ is one of the laws of life that someone has to pay the price of sin. God can and does forgive, but not even He can free us from the consequences of what we have done. It is the glory of the Christian faith that, just as Jesus Christ took upon Himself the sins of all, so there are those who in love are prepared to help pay for the consequences of the sins of those who are dear to them. Christianity never entitled anyone to default on debts. Onesimus must have stolen from Philemon, as well as run away from him. If he had not helped himself to Philemon's money, it is difficult to see how he could ever have covered the long road to Rome. Paul writes with his own hand that he will be responsible and will repay in full.

It is interesting to note that this is an exact instance of a *cheirographon*, the kind of acknowledgment met in Colossians 2:14. This is *a handwriting against Paul*, an obligation voluntarily accepted and signed.[51]

**William Barclay**

---

[51]The Letters to Timothy, Titus, and Philemon 3rd ed. (Westminster John Knox Press) pp. 319-320.

## KEY QUESTIONS

1. Who was Philemon and where did he live?

2. What information in the letter suggests that Onesimus was a slave who had run away from Philemon?

3. What difference should the salvation of Onesimus have made to his relationship with Philemon?

4. Should Paul have condemned slavery in this letter or in his other letter? Explain your answer.